Vegetarian
Indian

Vegetarian Indian

Shehzad Husain

Photography by Steve Baxter

ACKNOWLEDGEMENTS
Art Director **Jacqui Small**
Executive Art Editor **Penny Stock**
Designer **Louise Leffler**
Executive Editor **Susan Haynes**
Editors **Janice Anderson, Elsa Petersen-Schepelern, Kathy Steer**
Production Controller **Melanie Frantz**
Photographer **Steve Baxter**
Home Economist **Annie Nichols**
Stylist **Helen Payne**

Published in the USA 1995 by JG Press
Distributed by World Publications, Inc.

The JG Press imprint is a trademark of
JG Press, Inc.
455 Somerset Avenue
North Dighton, MA 02764

Library of Congress Cataloging in Publication Data available on request

ISBN 1-57215-115-3

Produced by Mandarin Offset
Printed and bound in China
NOTES

Eggs should be medium unless otherwise stated.

Milk should be whole unless otherwise stated.

Fresh herbs should be used unless otherwise stated.
If unavailable use dried herbs as an alternative but halve the quantities stated.

Ovens should be preheated to the specified temperature – if using a convection oven,
follow the manufacturer's instructions for adjusting the time and the temperature.

Many Indian dishes are suitable for vegans, who should avoid recipes containing eggs,
cream or milk, yogurt or panir, and use vegetable ghee instead of butter or clarified butter.
Many recipes, other than those containing cracked wheat (page 35), wheat flour and other
wheat products, and chapati flour (made of whole wheat flour), are suitable for those on a
gluten-free diet. Gram flour or besun, in particular, is suitable since it is made from lentils.
Indian vegetarian meals can be adapted for any members of the family who are not
vegetarians simply by adding another curry dish containing fish, poultry or meat.
Recipes serve 4, if served as part of a meal comprising several dishes.

All the jellies, jams and preserves should be processed in a
boiling water-bath canner according to the USDA guidelines.

ILLUSTRATION, *page 2: Indian breads, from the top, Besun Ki Roti
(recipe page 103) and Chapati (recipe page 102).*

Contents

Tamarind

Doodhi

Okra

Betel Leaf

Baby Eggplant

Tinday

Red Chiles

Cilantro

Green Chile

Karela (Bitter Gourd)

Green Mango

Doodhi

Fenugreek

Curry Leaves

Introduction

Vegetarian cooking in India is very highly developed, with a tradition going back thousands of years. It is largely based on religious principles. The major religious groups in the Indian subcontinent include Hindus, Muslims, Buddhists, Jains, Parsees, Sikhs, Jews and Christians. Many of these religions follow special dietary laws; Muslims and Jews do not eat pork, while Hindus never eat beef and rarely pork. Buddhists, some Hindu castes and Jains all have a long tradition of vegetarianism. Certain areas, such as Gujarat, Tamil Nadu and Kerala, are particularly well known for the quality of their vegetarian dishes.

Indian vegetarian cooking provides a wide variety of tastes. Its nutritional values are unsurpassed, and its variety is almost limitless, coming as it does from areas as diverse as the high Himalayas of Kashmir in the far north to the palm-fringed beaches of Kerala in the south, from the red deserts of Rajastan in the west to the jungles of Orissa in the east.

You will find in this book dishes from every corner of this huge and diverse country and recipes for the grandest and most sophisticated dinner party and for the most casual of take-out snacks. In fact, India can be said to have virtually invented fast food – pakoras, samosas and chaat have been the "eat-and-run" food of millions.

When serving an Indian meal, always provide more than one dish. Main vegetable curries should be accompanied by rice and/or bread, a dhaal (lentil) dish, one or more chutneys or pickles and perhaps a salad or raita. This will result in a meal which is nutritionally complete as well as delicious. You may find that some people like their dishes less spicy than others – for them, just decrease the quantity of chiles in the recipe.

The book is divided into courses, which is familiar to the western style of eating. In India, however, all the dishes would be served at the same time. They are placed in the middle of the table, and the diners help themselves according to their taste and appetite.

In the north, breads such as naan and rotis are the staple foods, while in the south, rice is the basis of every meal. In addition, I have included a chapter on "curries" although in India there is no such thing! "Curry," however, is how people in the west think of "main course" dishes in Indian cooking, so curry it is!

COOKING AND EATING VEGETARIAN FOOD

Cupboard items

Your basic stock of spices should include fresh ginger and garlic, chile powder, turmeric, cardamom, black pepper, ground coriander and cumin. The powdered spices will keep in airtight containers, carefully labelled, while the ginger and garlic will keep for seven to ten days in the refrigerator. Other useful items, to be acquired as your repertoire increases, are cumin seeds (black and white), onion seeds, mustard seeds, cloves, cinnamon, dried red chiles, fenugreek, vegetable ghee and garam masala, a mixture of spices that can either be bought ready-made or made at home in quantity for use whenever required. The Ingredients section on page 10 describes many of these items in greater detail.

Spices

It is a good idea, particularly if you are new to Indian cooking, to take out all the spices before you start cooking and keep them either on a plate or in small separate bowls. Chop onions and other vegetables before you start cooking.

Many of the recipes in this book call for ground spices, which are generally available in supermarkets as well as in Indian and Pakistani specialty stores. In India, cooks almost always buy whole spices and grind them at home, and there is no doubt that freshly ground spices make a

---

MAIL ORDER SOURCES

Dean & Deluca
560 Broadway, New York, NY 10012
tel: (1800) 221-7714

Foods of India
121 Lexington Avenue, New York, NY 10016
tel: (212) 683-4419

House of Spices
4605 North Sixth Street, North Philadelphia, PA 19140
tel: (215) 455-6870

India Gifts and Foods
1031 West Belmont Avenue, Chicago, Illinois 60650
tel: (312) 348-4392

noticeable difference to the end product. However, it is quicker and more convenient to use ground spices.

For some of the recipes in this book, the spices must be roasted. In India, this would be done on a *thawa* (see page 122), but a heavy-bottom skillet may be used instead. No water or oil is added to the spices; they are simply dry-roasted whole over a high heat while the pan is shaken to prevent them burning.

Ginger and Garlic

Both ginger and garlic are frequently used in curries. Since it takes time and effort to peel and chop them, I suggest you take about 8 ounces of each, soak them separately overnight (this makes them easy to peel), peel and grind separately in a food processor, adding a little water to form a pulp. The pulps can be stored separately in airtight containers in a cool place for a month or longer, to be used as you need them.

Yogurt

Always use plain unsweetened yogurt. When adding this ingredient to curries, I always whip it first with a fork so that it does not curdle, then I add it gradually. Yogurt helps to tenderize the other ingredients and give curry a thick, creamy texture. Raita – yogurt sauce – also complements most curries beautifully.

The secret of a good curry

The final color and texture of a curry will depend on how well you browned the onions in the first stage. This requires patience, especially if you are cooking a large quantity. Heat the oil, add the onions, then reduce the heat slightly so that the onions become golden without burning, and stir them gently with a wooden spoon or spatula as they cook.

Once this is done, add the spices, vegetables or other ingredients of the curry you are making and mix and coat by *bhoono-ing* (stirring and cooking in gentle semicircular movements, scraping the bottom of the pan). This is essential for a good end-result. When you have done this you should taste the food and adjust the seasoning according to your own palate. Remember that the recipes are only guidelines, not prescriptions, so you do not have to follow them rigidly.

Thickening sauces

In Indian cooking, flour is very rarely used to thicken sauces. Instead, Indian cooks rely on onions and spices (such as ginger, garlic or powdered coriander) to produce a thick brown sauce.

Making a baghaar (*seasoned oil dressing*)

As far as I know, this dressing is used only in Indian cooking. Oil or clarified butter is heated to a very high temperature without burning, and spices, onions and herbs are dropped into the oil, immediately changing color and becoming very aromatic. The seasoned oil is then removed from the heat and poured over the dish – often a cooked dhaal or vegetables – like a dressing. Sometimes raw food is added to the heated oil, to be sautéed or simmered. You will find instructions for baghaar in the relevant recipes.

Freezing Indian food

The good thing about Indian food is that most of it freezes well, with very little loss of flavor. The potato is an exception, though, as it becomes mushy when cooked and frozen in a curry. If you are planning to cook and freeze a dish containing potato, leave out the potato and add it on the day you serve the dish.

To reheat on the day, defrost the dish thoroughly at room temperature for a few hours and then reheat as appropriate; the best ways to reheat a thawed curry are either in an oven, in a saucepan over a gentle heat on top of the stove, or under a broiler, depending on the nature of the dish. Some dishes may be shallow-fried, but I find this makes the food a little too greasy. A microwave oven is, of course, the latest answer to thawing and reheating frozen dishes.

PRESENTATION

There are few rules about presenting Indian food, but if you are entertaining keep in mind which serving dishes you plan to use for each recipe, and do not neglect the final decorative touches – the fresh cilantro leaves or the chopped chile garnishes – that make the food look so appetizing. Curries and dhaal are best served in large, deep dishes, rice is piled on flat oval dishes and raita (yogurt sauce) is best served in a bowl or sauce boat. Breads such as chapatis, paratas or puris should be served on a plate wrapped in tinfoil to keep them warm for as long as possible. Pickles, chutneys and kachumbers (fruits or vegetables with spices in lemon juice) are eaten in small portions, so it is best to put them in small bowls, each with a teaspoon in them, so that people do not take large helpings. In any case some pickles can be very hot and are not intended to be eaten on their own or in large quantities.

Guests usually help themselves from the serving dishes. Rice is placed in the center of the dinner plate, leaving some room for the curries, which are never put on top of the rice. It is not necessary to help yourself to everything on the table at once.

Though you may wish to provide a cruet set for the dinner table, it is a mistake for anyone to add salt before tasting, because the cook will always have added it with all the other spices during cooking. Garnishes, such as cilantro leaves and green chiles, are best if fresh, though they may be prepared in advance and kept frozen in plastic bags or small freezer containers for convenience. Do not wash the cilantro before freezing it; just rinse it under a cold tap before use. Cilantro is easy to grow outdoors, and I have been reasonably successful growing it on the window sill; it is worthwhile growing your own cilantro – in case it is not always easy to find. Other attractive and inexpensive garnishes include slices of onions separated into rings, tomatoes and lemon wedges.

By contrast, a special way of decorating savory dishes or desserts is to use *varq* (beaten silver leaf, which is edible). This custom probably started with the Moguls, seeking to intrigue their guests at palace banquets, and is reserved for special occasions because it is very expensive. A dessert decorated with *varq* certainly looks beautiful, and is bound to impress your guests. It provides a talking point, but since it is real silver, it may not be very pleasant for people with fillings in their teeth.

Finally, if you want to clear your home of cooking smells after cooking Indian food, try lighting up a few incense sticks (*agarbathis*) about an hour before the guests are due. I find these are more effective than air fresheners, and they come in various fragrances, including jasmine and rose.

PLANNING MEALS

The dishes you choose will depend upon the occasion. For a dinner party, for example, a biryani or khitchri would make a very good centerpiece, though for a family meal you might prefer something less elaborate. The important thing to bear in mind is that protein should always be included, perhaps panir, or a bean or pea; lentil dishes, usually served as dhaal, are good complements for most vegetarian curries. I have indicated in each recipe whether the curry is "wet," that is with a sauce, or "dry," and this should help you to combine textures for a varied table.

Accompaniments such as chutneys and kachumbers are not a must, but I feel they perk up a meal; raitas are used to cool a hot curry or to freshen the palate. A typical vegetarian meal might consist of a vegetable curry, a lentil dish, a kachumber or chutney, rice and/or bhajias, followed by dessert. Usually, dishes are all served together, except for the dessert, following no particular order as in other cuisines – but of course this is up to you.

AN ABC OF INGREDIENTS

Asafetida
A pale yellow spice with a strong, distinctive flavor, used in small quantities to enhance other flavors in a dish.

Aamchoor
Sour-tasting mango powder made from dried raw mangoes. It is sold in jars.

Ata
see Whole wheat flour.

Besun
see Gram flour.

Bhoonay chanay
Dried-roasted chick peas.

Bitter gourd (*karela*)
A bitter-tasting gourd with a very knobbly skin. They should be peeled and salted or blanched before cooking to reduce the bitter flavor.

Bundi
Small, round, pearl-sized drops made from green lentil flour, usually soaked in water before use.

Cardamom (*elaichi*)
This spice, native to India, is considered the second most expensive (after saffron). The pods can be used with or without their husks and have a slightly pungent but very aromatic taste. They come in three varieties: green, white and black. The green and white pods can be used in both sweet and savory dishes or to flavor rice; the black pods are used only in savory dishes.

Cassia
see Cinnamon.

Cayenne pepper
see Chile powder.

Chana dhaal
Very similar in appearance to moong dhaal (yellow split peas) – this lentil has slightly less shiny grains. It is used as a binding agent.

Chana dhaal flour
see Gram flour.

Chapati flour
see Whole wheat flour.

Chile powder (*laal mirch*) or cayenne pepper
Powdered dried red chiles. It is a very fiery spice that should be used with caution.

Chiles, dried red (*sabath sookhi laal mirch*)
These pods, available whole or crushed, are extremely fiery and should be used with caution; their effect can be toned down slightly by removing the seeds. Dried chiles are usually sautéed in oil before use.

Chiles, fresh green (*hari mirch*)
Very aromatic in flavor, these are used both in cooking, and as a garnish. Though now so closely identified with

Garam Masala

Fennel Seeds

Brown Chick peas

Saffron

Mild Madras Curry Powder

Pomegranate Seeds

Masoor Dhaal

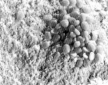

Moong Dhaal

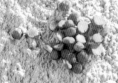

Chana Dhaal

Whole Masoor Dhaal

Turmeric

Whole Urid Dhaal

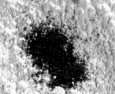

Cayenne Pepper

Cinnamon Bark

Poppy Seeds

Nutmeg

Black Mustard Seeds

Curry Leaves

Dried Chiles

Cloves

White Cardamom

Fenugreek Seeds

Mustard Seeds

Cumin

Mustard Seeds

Black Whole Cardamom

Green Cardamom

Coriander Seeds

Indian cooking, they were not introduced to the country until the 16th century by the Portuguese. The seeds, which are the hottest part, may be removed if desired, by slitting the chile down the middle. Never touch the face, especially the eyes or nose, during or after handling chiles; even after washing your hands it will sting.

Cinnamon (*dhalchini*)
One of the earliest-known spices, cinnamon comes from the bark of a tree grown mainly in Sri Lanka. It has an aromatic and sweet flavor. Sold both in powdered form and as sticks. The bark of the tree which cinnamon comes from is sold as Cassia bark.

Cloves (*laung*)
Used to flavor many sweet and savory dishes; usually added whole. A whole clove is sometimes used to seal a betel leaf for serving after an Indian meal (see Paan).

Coconut (*khopra or narial*)
Used to flavor sweet or savory dishes, fresh coconut can often be bought in supermarkets. Shredded coconut and coconut milk are also available and for most dishes make acceptable substitutes. Coconut is sometimes toasted before cooking (as for spices, see page 8).

Cilantro, fresh (*hara dhania*)
A fragrant herb used as an ingredient and as a garnish.

Coriander seeds (*dhania*)
This aromatic spice has a pungent, slightly lemony flavor. The seeds are used widely, either coarsely ground or powdered, in meat, fish and poultry dishes.

Corn oil
Less fattening than other oils, especially clarified butter, and also odourless, this is my preferred cooking oil.

Cumin, ground (*safaid zeera*)
A rather musty-smelling spice in its raw state, widely used for flavoring lentils and vegetable curries. Its flavor comes into its own when roasted or sautéed.

Cumin seeds (*shah zeera*)
Black cumin seeds, which have a strong aromatic flavor, are used to flavor curries and rice. White cumin seeds cannot be used as a substitute.

Curry leaves (*kari patta*)
Similar in appearance to bay leaves but very different in flavor. Available fresh (occasionally) or dried, they are used to flavor lentil dishes and vegetable curries.

Doodhi (*kaddu*)
A vegetable – a member of the squash family. It is shaped rather like a curved zucchini and is generally pale green in color. Marrow, squash or zucchini can be substituted.

Fennel seeds (*sonfe*)
Similar to white cumin, these have a sweet taste and are used to flavor certain curries. They can also be chewed (as betel nut and cardamom are) after a spicy meal.

Fenugreek (*methi*)
The flavor of the whole, dried, flat yellow seeds, a little bitter in taste, improves when they are lightly sautéed. Fresh fenugreek, sold in bunches, has very small leaves and is used to flavor both meat and vegetarian dishes.

Garam masala
A mixture of spices which can either be made up at home from freshly ground spices or bought ready-made. There is no set formula, but a typical mixture might include black cumin seeds, peppercorns, cloves, cinnamon and black cardamom. To make your own mixture, grind together a 1-inch piece cinnamon stick, 3 cloves, 3 black peppercorns, 2 black cardamoms (with husks removed) and 2 teaspoons black cumin seeds. If you like, multiply the quantities, grind, and store in an airtight jar for future use.

Garlic (*lassun*)
This very useful flavoring is frequently used in curries, especially with ginger. It can be puréed in large quantities in a food processor and kept in an airtight container in the refrigerator (see page 9). Whole garlic cloves are sometimes added to lentil dishes.

Ghee (*clarified butter*)
There are two kinds: pure (a dairy product) and vegetable. Though it was once a matter of pride to be able to claim that everything served in one's household was cooked in pure clarified butter, it is in fact very high in cholesterol, so from the health viewpoint it is better to use vegetable ghee or vegetable oil wherever possible (the majority of curries are cooked in oil). To make pure clarified butter at home, melt 1 cup (2 sticks) butter in a heavy saucepan and allow to simmer for 10–12 minutes. Once the milky white froth has turned golden, strain (preferably through muslin or cheesecloth) and store in a jar.

Ginger root (*adrak, fresh ginger, green ginger*)
One of the most popular flavorings in India and also one of the oldest, ginger is an important ingredient in many curries. It should always be peeled before use and can be puréed in a food processor (see page 9). Dried powdered ginger (*sontt*) is also useful to have in your cupboard.

Gram flour (*besun or chana dhaal flour*)
Made from lentils, gram flour is used to make pakoras, and can also be used as a binding agent. A combination of gram flour and ordinary whole wheat flour (*ata*, or chapati flour) makes a delicious Indian bread called *Besun Ki Roti* (see recipe, page 103). This kind of flour is also very useful for people who are allergic to gluten, a component of all wheat products.

Kaddu
see Doodhi.

Karela
see Bitter gourd.

Kewra water

This is the essence of pandanus or screwpine, used to flavor sweet dishes and sometimes rice. It is sold in small bottles. Its scent is rather reminiscent of vanilla, and a little vanilla essence may be substituted.

Mace

see Nutmeg.

Masoor dhaal

Small, round and pale orange in color, these split lentils are stocked by all supermarkets, labelled simply "lentils" or "red lentils."

Mooli

From the same family as the radish; long, rather like a cucumber, and white, mooli has a lovely flavor and a crunchy texture. It goes well with carrot.

Moong dhaal

This is a tear drop-shaped yellow split lentil, more popular in northern India than in the south.

Mustard oil

Often used in Bengali dishes, especially for cooking fish.

Mustard seeds (*sarson ke beenji rai*)

These small round seeds, either black or yellow, are rather sharp in flavor. They are used in curries and pickles.

Nutmeg (*jaifal*)

Nutmeg, a native of Indonesia, is sweet and aromatic. Mace, with its slightly more subtle flavor, is the lacy covering on the nutmeg kernel.

Onion seeds (*kalongi*)

Black in color and triangular in shape, these are used for both pickles and vegetable curries.

Paan

Betel leaf wrapped around calcium paste, cardamom and fennel seeds, etc., and held together with a clove and sometimes covered with *varq*. Served at the end of the meal as a mouth-freshener. It may contain tobacco, in which case it can be addictive. It can be bought or made at home.

Paprika

This powder, made from dried sweet red pepper, is known as a hot-flavored spice, though it is much less fiery than chile pepper. Paprika is not used much in Indian cookery.

Pepper

Whenever possible, use freshly ground black pepper in Indian cooking.

Pistachio nuts

Widely used in Indian desserts, these are not the salty ones, but the shelled ones sold in packets at all Indian and Pakistani specialty stores.

Poppy seeds (*khush khush*)

These dried whole seeds are always better when roasted. They are used, often whole, to flavor curries. Although they are from the opium poppy, they do not contain opium.

Rosewater

This is used mainly to flavor certain sweetmeats.

Saffron (*zafran*)

The world's most expensive spice has a uniquely beautiful flavor and fragrance. Made from the stigmas of the saffron crocus, native to Asia Minor, each 1 lb of saffron needs 60,000 stigmas. Fortunately, only a small quantity is needed to flavor or color a dish, whether sweet or savory. Saffron is sold as strands or in powder form.

Sesame seeds (*thill*)

Whole, flat, cream-colored seeds, these are used to flavor curries. When ground, sesame seeds can also be made into chutney.

Set

A spice mixture.

Sev

Very fine gram flour strands, used in *bhel poori*, which can be bought in Indian and Pakistani specialty stores.

Sontt

see Ginger root.

Tamarind (*imli*)

The dried pods of the tamarind, or Indian date. They are sour tasting and very sticky. Tamarind has to be soaked in hot water to extract the flavor. Though it is much stronger than lemon, lemon is often used as a substitute. Nowadays tamarind can be bought in paste form in jars: mix with a little water to bring it to a runny consistency.

Toor dhaal

Split pigeon peas; larger and more yellow than moong dhaal (see above).

Turmeric (*haled*)

This bright yellow, bitter-tasting spice is sold ground. It is used mainly for color, rather than flavor.

Urid dhaal

Though very similar in shape and size to moong dhaal, this lentil is white and a little drier when cooked. It is popular in northern India.

Urid dhaal flour

This very fine white flour is used for vadde (deep-fried dumplings – recipe on page 111), and for dosai (Indian rice pancakes).

Varq

Edible silver leaf used for decoration. It is very delicate and should be handled carefully. It can be bought in sheets from Indian or Pakistani specialty stores, though you may have to order it in advance.

Whole wheat flour (*ata*)

Chapati flour, available at any Indian or Pakistani specialty store, is used to make chapatis, paratas and puris. Ordinary whole wheat flour may also be used for Indian breads, very well sifted.

Appetizers and Snacks

The dishes in this chapter may be served
Indian-style — that is, at the same time as the
curry and lentil dishes in a meal — or western-style, as something to whet the appetite while the main courses are being
completed. Either way, they are delicious. Many of them
also make perfect snacks, or form
the basis for light, middle-of-the-day meals.

Baby Potatoes in Mint

These can be served as an appetizer with a crisp salad (see pages 111–113) – but they are also perfect as an accompaniment for other curry and bean and lentil dishes. The flavors also go very well with western vegetarian dishes. Choose any small potato variety, the yellow, waxy, French salad potatoes, or the delightfully named Pink Fir Apples.

20–25 BABY POTATOES

4 OUNCES (1 STICK) UNSALTED BUTTER

½ TEASPOON GARLIC PULP

3 GREEN CHILES, FINELY CHOPPED

3 TABLESPOONS CHOPPED FRESH MINT

3 TABLESPOONS CHOPPED FRESH CILANTRO

1½ TEASPOONS SALT

3 TABLESPOONS LEMON JUICE

Wash and slice the potatoes thickly, then boil them in lightly salted water until they are soft but not mushy, so they retain their shape.

Melt the butter in a small saucepan and add the garlic, green chiles, mint, cilantro, salt and lemon juice. Blend together in the pan before pouring the mixture over the potatoes.

Serve immediately.

Baked Baby Potato Chaat

This makes a delicious appetizer. You should serve about three to four per person. In India, there are shops devoted to selling various kinds of chaats. You mix chaat spices to your own individual taste and sprinkle them over the food. Chaat spices include salt, chile powder, ginger and ground, roasted cumin seeds. Chaats are delicious when eaten with glasses of lassi (see pages 26 and 120). Although lemon juice may be used instead of tamarind, the latter is such an intrinsic part of this dish that it's better not to replace it.

16 BABY POTATOES

¾ CUP BOILING WATER

8 OUNCES RED TAMARIND BLOCK

3 TABLESPOONS TOMATO SAUCE

1 TEASPOON CHILE POWDER

1 TEASPOON SALT

1 TEASPOON GINGER POWDER

2 TABLESPOONS SUGAR

1 TABLESPOON CHOPPED FRESH MINT

1 TABLESPOON CHOPPED FRESH CILANTRO

2 TABLESPOONS PLAIN YOGURT, WHISKED

2 TABLESPOONS WATER

TO GARNISH

1 SMALL ONION, DICED

1 TABLESPOON CHOPPED FRESH CILANTRO

2 GREEN CHILES, CHOPPED

1 TOMATO, DICED

Wash and prick the potatoes and bake in a hot oven, 400°F, until cooked.

Meanwhile, pour the boiling water over the tamarind block. Once the water is cool, squeeze the pulp out of the tamarind and push it through a strainer. Blend this with the tomato sauce, and then mix in the chile powder, salt, ginger powder, sugar, mint and cilantro.

Pour the tamarind sauce over the potatoes and garnish with the diced onion, cilantro, chopped chiles and diced tomato.

For the yogurt sauce, mix the yogurt and water together in a small bowl, adding a little salt to taste. Serve the chaat cold with yogurt sauce poured over the top.

PREVIOUS PAGES: *From left, Mixed Chaat with Tamarind Chutney (recipe page 26) and Fried Moong Dhaal (recipe page 22). There are special chaat shops in India – you choose your dish, then sprinkle it with chaat spices. Lassi, often tamarind-flavored, is traditionally drunk with chaat, so tamarind chutney is an appropriate accompaniment. Slightly salted Fried Moong Dhaal is good to nibble with drinks.*

RIGHT: *The potato is native to Peru, and was only discovered in 1534 by Pizarro, who brought it to Europe. It has been enthusiastically adopted by cooks all over the Indian subcontinent and has become a staple food in some areas, such as the high Himalayas. Illustrated from the top are Baby Potatoes in Mint (recipe above), Bombay Aloo (recipe on page 18), and Baked Baby Potato Chaat (recipe above, right).*

Bombay Aloo

Illustrated on the previous page, Bombay Aloo is one of the most popular potato dishes in the Indian culinary repertoire, especially in the west. It can be eaten as a snack or served as an appetizer with one of the salads from this book on pages 111–113. This recipe can be made with any small potato variety, but I like it very much with the little, waxy, yellow ones, sometimes sold simply as "Mediterranean potatoes," or salad potatoes. These will hold their shape better than the floury kind.

12–14 BABY POTATOES
2 TABLESPOONS TOMATO PASTE
1 TEASPOON GROUND CORIANDER
1 TEASPOON CHILE POWDER
1 TEASPOON SALT
1 TEASPOON SUGAR
2 TABLESPOONS LEMON JUICE
1 TABLESPOON OIL
½ TEASPOON MUSTARD SEEDS
6 CURRY LEAVES
1 TABLESPOON CHOPPED FRESH CILANTRO, TO GARNISH

Boil the baby potatoes with their skins on and cut them in half once they're cooked. Place on a serving dish.

Meanwhile, in a small bowl mix together the tomato paste, ground coriander, chile powder, salt, sugar and lemon juice.

Heat the oil in a small skillet over a medium heat and gently sauté the mustard seeds and curry leaves. Reduce the heat and add the tomato paste and spice mixture to the pan. Cook for about 1 minute then pour the hot mixture over the potatoes. Mix in carefully. Before serving, garnish the dish with chopped fresh cilantro.

VARIATION

Bombay Aloo with Panir

Panir (see recipe on page 74) is a delicious addition to this dish. Just before serving, slice the panir, sauté it lightly in clarified butter, then add to the other ingredients.

To serve, finely slice 2 green chiles and scatter over, then garnish with sprigs of mint.

Masala Potato Wedges

A great snack at any time of the day, and also excellent as an appetizer with a crisp green salad, or as a nibble with drinks (serve it with the yogurt dip described below). This dish can be teamed with the Spicy Mushroom and Cilantro Omelet on page 24 as a light lunch.

3 POTATOES, CUT LENGTHWISE INTO QUARTERS
2 TABLESPOONS WATER
2 TABLESPOONS TOMATO PASTE
3 TABLESPOONS LEMON JUICE
1 TEASPOON SALT
1 TEASPOON CHILE POWDER
1½ TEASPOONS GROUND CORIANDER
1 TEASPOON GROUND CUMIN
1 TABLESPOON CHOPPED FRESH CILANTRO
2 TABLESPOONS CORN OIL

Boil the potatoes in lightly salted water until they are cooked, but still firm. Do not boil them until soft as they will be cooked again when coated in spices and roasted.

In a bowl, mix the water, tomato paste, lemon juice, salt and all the spices together to make a smooth paste. Pour over the potatoes, coating each one thoroughly but not too heavily.

Place the potato wedges in a large ovenproof dish and bake in a preheated oven, 350°F, for 20–25 minutes. Serve hot.

VARIATIONS

Masala Eggplant, Zucchini or Carrots

Cut small eggplants into wedges, or large ones into slices. Cut zucchinis into thick batons or carrots into smaller ones. Parboil the vegetables and proceed as in the main recipe.

Yogurt Sauce for Masala Potatoes, Eggplant, Zucchini or Carrots

Delicious with drinks – a selection of Masala Potato Wedges, Eggplant, Zucchini or Carrots served with yogurt sauce. Mix 4 ounces Greek or homemade yogurt with ½ teaspoon salt, 1 teaspoon sugar, 1 tablespoon chopped fresh cilantro leaves and 1–2 chopped fresh green chiles. Use 1 chile for a milder sauce and 2 if your guests like it spicy.

Vegetable Croquettes

Croquettes were first introduced into Indian cooking by Indian cooks working for British Raj households, in an attempt to approximate dishes familiar to Europeans. They are also made with meat, but this now-traditional vegetarian version is truly wonderful.

2 LARGE POTATOES

½ CUP PEAS

2 LARGE CARROTS, FINELY DICED

¼ CUP CORN

1 ONION, CHOPPED

1½ TEASPOONS GARAM MASALA

1 TEASPOON CHILE POWDER

2 RED CHILES, CHOPPED

2 TABLESPOONS CHOPPED FRESH CILANTRO

1½ TEASPOONS SALT

1 EGG, BEATEN (OPTIONAL)

4 CUPS BREAD CRUMBS

OIL FOR SHALLOW-FRYING

Cook the potatoes in boiling salted water until they are well cooked but not mushy. Mash and set aside.

Boil the peas, carrots, corn and onion together in lightly salted water. When they are all cooked, drain thoroughly and gently mash them down.

Mix all the vegetables with the garam masala, chile powder, red chiles, fresh cilantro and salt.

Taste for seasoning before breaking off small balls from the vegetable mixture, about the size of a golf ball, to form small croquettes in the palms of your hands.

Place the beaten egg, if using, in a shallow dish and the bread crumbs in another. Roll the croquettes first in beaten egg (optional), then in bread crumbs, coating them thoroughly.

Heat some oil in a skillet and shallow-fry the croquettes for about 1 minute, turning once.

Serve as an appetizer, accompaniment or snack.

Potato and Onion Croquettes
(Aloo Aur Pyaaz Kay Croquettes)

"Aloo" is the Hindi and Urdu word for potato – worthwhile remembering if you're trying to find your way around a menu in an Indian restaurant. These little "potato balls" can be served as an appetizer, or even with drinks. To make the ginger pulp, either shred it finely, or purée the fresh root in a spice grinder, or sprinkle it with a little salt and mash it to a pulp with the point of a heavy knife.

4 LARGE POTATOES, PEELED AND DICED

1 TEASPOON GINGER PULP

2 TEASPOONS MANGO POWDER

2 TEASPOONS CHILE POWDER

3 GREEN CHILES, CHOPPED

3 TABLESPOONS CHOPPED FRESH MINT

4 TABLESPOONS CHOPPED FRESH CILANTRO

2 TEASPOONS SALT

¼ CUP CORN OIL

2 ONIONS, DICED

¼ TEASPOON ONION SEEDS

2 EGGS, LIGHTLY BEATEN

4 CUPS BREAD CRUMBS

Boil the diced potatoes in lightly salted water and, when cooked, mash them, leaving some lumpy pieces.

Blend together the ginger pulp, mango powder, chile powder, chopped green chiles, mint, cilantro and salt in either a spice grinder or food processor. Add this mixture to the mashed potato and set aside.

Heat 2 tablespoons of oil in a skillet and sauté the onions with the onion seeds until golden brown. Remove the pan from the heat and let cool. Using a slotted spoon, remove the onions and pour onto the potato mixture, and with your hands, mix together thoroughly.

Break off small balls from the potato and onion mixture. Pat them in the palms of your hands to form flat, round shapes about 1 inch thick. You should get 10–12 croquettes.

Dip the potato croquettes in beaten eggs and then roll them in the bread crumbs, coating them thoroughly. Heat the remaining oil in a skillet and shallow-fry the croquettes over a medium heat in 2 or 3 batches until golden brown, turning them at least once during cooking.

Serve hot either as an appetizer or as a side dish.

Buttered Vegetables

These vegetables make an excellent accompaniment to almost anything – even a fried egg.

2 ZUCCHINI, SLICED (ABOUT ¼-INCH THICK)

2 CARROTS, SLICED

½ CAULIFLOWER, BROKEN INTO FLOWERETS

1 SWEET GREEN PEPPER, DESEEDED AND SLICED

4 OUNCES (1 STICK) BUTTER

1 TEASPOON SALT

1 TABLESPOON CHOPPED FRESH CILANTRO

1 TEASPOON GARLIC PULP

1 TEASPOON CRUSHED DRIED RED CHILES

Place the vegetables in a large serving dish. Put the butter with the salt, cilantro, garlic and crushed red chiles in a small saucepan. Melt over a high heat then pour over the vegetables. Toss and serve immediately.

Creamy Buttered Saag Panir

A sumptuous variation of the recipe above, which can also be served as part of a main course.

2 LB FRESH SPINACH, WASHED AND CHOPPED FINELY

12–14 CUBES PANIR, 1-INCH SQUARE

4 OUNCES (1 STICK) BUTTER

¼ TEASPOON ONION SEEDS

4 CURRY LEAVES

½ TEASPOON GARLIC PULP

½ TEASPOON POWDERED GINGER

1 TEASPOON CHILE POWDER

½ TEASPOON SALT

⅔ CUP LIGHT CREAM

1 TABLESPOON LEMON JUICE

2 FRESH RED CHILES, CHOPPED

Place the spinach in a saucepan with just the water clinging to the leaves and steam until wilted.

Heat 1 ounce (¼ stick) of the butter in a small skillet and sauté the cubes of panir until they are lightly browned on all sides. Put the spinach and panir in a small serving dish and mix carefully.

Melt the remaining butter in a small pan, add the remaining ingredients except the lemon juice and chiles, then pour over the spinach and panir. Sprinkle with lemon juice, scatter the chopped red chiles over them, then serve.

Mushroom and Leek Bhajias

"First cousins" to pakoras, bhajias can be made from many different kinds of vegetables. These make an ideal snack any time of the day. Serve them with Spicy Tomato Ketchup on page 117.

2 CUPS GRAM FLOUR

1 TEASPOON SALT

½ TEASPOON BAKING SODA

1 TEASPOON POMEGRANATE SEEDS

1 TEASPOON WHITE CUMIN SEEDS

1½ TEASPOONS CRUSHED RED CHILES

¼ TEASPOON TURMERIC

3 GREEN CHILES

3 CUPS MUSHROOMS, SLICED

2 LEEKS, CLEANED AND SLICED

1 TEASPOON CRUSHED CORIANDER SEEDS

2 TABLESPOONS CHOPPED FRESH CILANTRO

WATER TO MIX

CORN OIL FOR DEEP-FRYING

Sift the gram flour, salt and baking soda into a bowl. Add the pomegranate seeds, white cumin seeds and crushed red chiles. Mix together and then add turmeric, green chiles, mushrooms, leeks, coriander seeds, and fresh cilantro.

Add sufficient water to make a batter, about the consistency of a pancake mixture (like heavy cream). Set aside for about 10 minutes.

Meanwhile, heat the oil either in a karahi or a deep skillet to 350°F, or until a cube of bread browns in 30 seconds. Using a tablespoon, drop spoonfuls of the batter mixture into the hot oil and cook quickly. When each bhajia looks quite firm at the bottom, turn it over with a slotted spoon.

Reduce the heat to medium if the oil becomes too hot.

Once the bhajias are cooked right through, remove them and drain on absorbent paper towels to absorb excess oil.

Serve the bhajias hot, ideally as they are being cooked, with spicy ketchup.

VARIATION

Onion Bhajias

One of the best-known Indian appetizers or snacks. Substitute 3 cups of sliced onions for the mushrooms and leeks, and proceed as in the main recipe.

LEFT: *Above, Buttered Vegetables (recipe above, left) and Mushroom and Leek Bhajias (recipe above). Bhajias can be made from many different vegetables, including onions (see variation, above) and zucchini, cauliflower, sweet peppers and chiles (see recipe on page 44).*

Dosai

A southern dish now popular all over India. Serve with chutney or spicy vegetable filling (masala dosai). Dosa flour can be substituted for the rice and dhaal.

1¼ CUPS RICE OR GROUND RICE
½ CUP URID DHAAL OR URID DHAAL FLOUR
1 TEASPOON SALT
4 TABLESPOONS CORN OR VEGETABLE OIL

Pick over the urid dhaal and discard any stones or twigs. Soak rice and dhaal for at least 3 hours, then grind smoothly. Add water to give a batter-like consistency. If using ground rice and urid dhaal flour – or dosa flour – just mix with water to a similar consistency. Set aside for a further 3 hours to ferment.

Heat 1 tablespoon of oil in a large, preferably non-stick pan. Pour in the rice mixture, and tilt to spread the batter over the base. Cover and cook for 2 minutes. Remove the lid, turn over the dosa and cook for a further 2 minutes, pouring a little oil around the edge. Serve with chutney.

Fried Moong Dhaal

Moong dhaal is made from dried mung beans – those same mung beans which produce the bean sprouts used in Chinese and other Oriental cuisines. Both varieties, brown and yellow, are extremely popular in Indian cooking. The yellow one has been husked and split, the brown just split. In this recipe, the moong dhaal is deep-fried until crisp. It is just salted so it has a subtle taste and is ideal for serving with drinks.

1 CUP YELLOW MOONG DHAAL
5 CUPS WATER
1¼ CUPS CORN OIL
1 TEASPOON SALT

Wash the moong dhaal thoroughly and soak it in the water for several hours, ideally overnight.

Drain off the liquid and leave the moong dhaal aside in a strainer so all the liquid is drained off.

When thoroughly drained, heat the oil in a karahi or a deep skillet and start cooking the dhaal in small quantities.

Using a slotted spoon, lift the cooked moong dhaal out of the pan and drain it on absorbent paper towels.

When all the dhaal is cooked, sprinkle salt on top and serve. When cooled, dhaal may be stored in plastic bags in a cupboard for 2–3 weeks.

Illustrated on page 15.

Bombay Mix
(Chewra)

Bombay Mix consists of split peas with flaked rice, cashews and raisins. Mixes like this are served at any time of day, with drinks or tea. You can make a large quantity and store in an airtight container as a change from potato chips. If you have any difficulty finding curry leaves, just leave them out.

1¼ CUPS CORN OIL
½ TEASPOON ONION SEEDS
½ TEASPOON FENNEL SEEDS
6 CURRY LEAVES
⅓ CUP PEAS
1⅓ CUPS FLAKED RICE (PAWA)
¼ CUP CASHEW NUTS
¼ CUP RAISINS
⅓ CUP SUGAR
1 TEASPOON SALT
1 TEASPOON CHILE POWDER

Heat the oil in a saucepan and sauté the onion seeds, fennel seeds and curry leaves. Addthe peas. Add the flaked rice and cook until crisp and golden (making sure the mixture doesn't burn). Using a slotted spoon, remove the mixture from the pan and put on a small tray lined with paper towels to absorb any excess oil. Tip the mixture into a bowl. Sauté the cashew nuts in the remaining oil, remove with a slotted spoon and mix with the flaked rice. Then add the raisins, sugar, salt and chile powder and mix well. Serve Bombay Mix immediately or store in an airtight container.

Deep-fried Okra

Okra is known as "bhindi" in India, and "ladies' fingers" in parts of the Middle East. It is a favorite ingredient in vegetarian Indian cooking. Okra is a well-traveled vegetable – you find it also in American Creole cookery. Sautéed as in this recipe, it makes a delicious, crispy accompaniment to any meal, and an interesting snack on its own or with drinks. When choosing okra, make sure the pods are as fresh and young as possible. Check the stalk end, which should be green and firm. The pods themselves should also be quite firm. Bend them a little, and reject them if they show any signs of flabbiness.

1 LB OKRA

1¼ CUPS OIL

½ TEASPOON SALT

TO GARNISH

2–3 SPRIGS FRESH CILANTRO

4 LEMON WEDGES

Wash entire okras and dry them thoroughly on absorbent paper towels. Trim and cut them into ½-inch thick pieces.

Heat the oil in a karahi or deep skillet and cook the okra in batches until crisp. Remove with a slotted spoon and drain on absorbent paper towels.

Once all the okra is cooked, transfer to a serving dish, sprinkle with salt and serve garnished with the cilantro sprigs and lemon wedges.

VARIATION

Deep-fried Cauliflower and Potato

For the okra, substitute 2 cups potatoes, peeled and diced into ½-inch cubes and about 2 cups cauliflower, broken into small flowerets. Cook the vegetables as in the main recipe, transfer to a serving dish, then sprinkle with 1 teaspoon white cumin seeds and garnish with fresh cilantro.

Spicy Vegetable Selection

This is a delicious mix of different vegetables – you can vary it according to which vegetables look freshest and juiciest at the time. However, I think that the sweet peppers are crucial to the mix, so don't leave them out on any account. They are available in wonderful colors these days, including yellow and purple. Don't feel that this recipe can only be used as an appetizer, though – it is also perfect served as a side dish other curries, and with Thali, the traditional South Indian dish on page 75.

2 MEDIUM ZUCCHINI

1 MEDIUM EGGPLANT

2 LARGE POTATOES

2 MEDIUM CARROTS

1 SWEET GREEN PEPPER, HALVED AND DESEEDED

1 SWEET RED PEPPER, HALVED AND DESEEDED

1 SWEET ORANGE PEPPER, HALVED AND DESEEDED

3 GREEN CHILES, FINELY CHOPPED

2 TABLESPOONS CHOPPED FRESH CILANTRO

1 TEASPOON GROUND CORIANDER

2 TEASPOONS MANGO POWDER

2 TABLESPOONS LEMON JUICE

1½ TEASPOONS SALT

2 TABLESPOONS OLIVE OIL

Cut all the vegetables into thick pieces: zucchini into 1-inch thick slices; eggplant into 1-inch thick slices; potatoes into wedges lengthwise; carrots into 1-inch thick pieces; peppers diced into large pieces.

Once all the vegetables are prepared, blanch the potatoes and carrots so they are cooked but not too soft and then transfer to an ovenproof dish.

Mix the green chiles, fresh cilantro, ground coriander, mango powder, lemon juice, salt and olive oil together in a small bowl. Pour over the vegetables and with a brush, spread the mixture over, coating the vegetables thoroughly.

Heat the broiler to the hottest temperature, lower it to medium and broil the vegetables, basting occasionally with the oil and spice mixture, for 7–10 minutes. Serve hot.

Spicy Mushroom and Cilantro Omelet

In India, omelets usually just have onion, chiles and cilantro as flavorings and are eaten mostly at breakfast or brunches. Do try this recipe with mushrooms as it is delicious, especially when served with Masala Potato Wedges (recipe page 18).

2 TOMATOES

1 SMALL ONION, FINELY CHOPPED

1 X 1-INCH PIECE FRESH GINGER, SHREDDED

1 TEASPOON CRUSHED DRIED RED CHILES

1 TABLESPOON CHOPPED FRESH CILANTRO

1 TEASPOON SALT

2 GREEN CHILES, COARSELY CHOPPED

4 MUSHROOMS, SLICED

4 EGGS, LIGHTLY BEATEN

2 TABLESPOONS CORN OIL

Cut the tops off the tomatoes and remove as much pulp as possible. Dice coarsely and place in a large mixing bowl.

Using a fork, thoroughly mix the onion, ginger, crushed red chiles, cilantro, salt and green chiles and then add to the diced tomatoes.

Add the sliced mushrooms, then the beaten eggs and whisk everything together.

Heat half the oil in a large skillet and add half of the egg mixture. Sauté until cooked, turning once. Remove the omelet from the pan and keep warm on a serving plate. Heat the remaining oil in the pan, add the remaining egg mixture and make a second omelet.

Serve the omelets with Masala Potato Wedges, if you like.

VARIATION

Omelet with Fresh Red Chiles or Sweet Peppers
For a very colorful version of this recipe, substitute 2 coarsely chopped red chiles for the green. If you prefer your omelet a little less spicy substitute finely diced sweet red pepper.

Thick Spicy Vegetable Soup

Soup was not very common in Indian cuisine. However, Indian cooks are now developing their own soup recipes, and this one is a delicious example. It is almost like a broth and is very warming on a cold winter day.

1 SMALL ONION

1 CARROT

2 MUSHROOMS

1 POTATO

¾ CUP PEAS

1 TEASPOON TOMATO PASTE

1¼ CUPS WATER

1 TABLESPOON CORN OIL

1 LARGE PINCH ONION SEEDS

½ TEASPOON GROUND CORIANDER

½ TEASPOON GARAM MASALA

½ TEASPOON CHILE POWDER

1 TEASPOON CHOPPED FRESH CILANTRO

1 TABLESPOON CORNSTARCH

2 TEASPOONS LEMON JUICE

4 TABLESPOONS LIGHT CREAM

1 TEASPOON SALT

FRESH CILANTRO SPRIGS, TO GARNISH

Peel and dice the onion, carrot, mushrooms and potato very finely and place in a large bowl.

Add the peas, mix in the tomato paste and pour in ⅔ cup of the water to loosen the mixture.

Heat the oil in a karahi or deep skillet and sauté the onion seeds until they turn a shade darker. Lower the heat, add the vegetable mixture and stir into the oil. Add the ground coriander, garam masala, chile powder and fresh cilantro.

Mix the cornstarch with the remaining water and pour onto the vegetables in the pan. Stir and cook for about 2 minutes, then pour in the lemon juice and mix thoroughly. Finally, stir in the cream and add salt to taste.

Transfer to a warmed serving dish and serve garnished with cilantro sprigs.

RIGHT: *From top, Thick Spicy Vegetable Soup (recipe above, right) is deliciously warming on a cold winter day, while Spicy Mushroom and Cilantro Omelet (recipe above), is an unusual variation on the more common Indian breakfast omelet and includes onion, chiles and cilantro. Substitute sweet red pepper for the chiles if you prefer a milder taste.*

Mixed Chaat with Tamarind Chutney

Chaat shops are very popular in India. Customers sprinkle chaat spices over their chosen dishes, while the delicious, cooling yogurt drink, lassi, flavored with tamarind, is the usual accompaniment. Here, that same fresh-tasting tamarind is used to make the chutney which accompanies the chaat.

1¼ CUPS PLAIN YOGURT

½ CUP WATER

2 TABLESPOONS SUGAR

1½ TEASPOONS SALT

2 POTATOES, COARSELY DICED

14 OUNCE CAN CHICK PEAS

PASTRY SQUARES

1½ CUPS SELF-RISING FLOUR

1 TEASPOON SALT

¼ TEASPOON WHITE CUMIN SEEDS

4 TABLESPOONS (½ STICK) BUTTER

WATER (SEE METHOD)

CORN OIL FOR DEEP-FRYING

TAMARIND CHUTNEY

6 OUNCES RED TAMARIND BLOCK

1¼ CUPS WATER

½ TEASPOON POWDERED GINGER

2 TABLESPOONS SUGAR

1 TEASPOON CHILE POWDER

1 TEASPOON SALT

2 TABLESPOONS TOMATO SAUCE

TO GARNISH

1 TABLESPOON CHOPPED FRESH CILANTRO

1 TABLESPOON PEANUTS

1 TABLESPOON SET (OPTIONAL)

Place the yogurt, water, sugar and salt together in a large bowl, whisk well and set aside. Boil the diced potato until soft, drain well and set aside. Drain the can of chick peas and add to the cooked potatoes.

To make the pastry squares, sift the flour and salt into a large mixing bowl. Mix in the cumin seeds and rub in the butter, using your fingertips. Add sufficient water to form a soft dough. Let the dough stand for about 10 minutes before rolling it out on a lightly floured surface to about ⅛ inch thick. Using a pastry cutter, cut the pastry into 1-inch squares. (You should get about 10–12 squares.) Set aside on a floured surface. To deep-fry the squares, heat sufficient oil in a skillet or karahi over a moderate heat and cook the squares in batches, turning them at least twice. When they are golden brown, remove from the pan with a slotted spoon and drain on paper towels.

To make the tamarind chutney, boil the tamarind in water for 7–10 minutes. Place the tamarind block in a strainer and press down with a spoon to form a thick pulp. Add a little water to make a thick sauce, then add the ginger, sugar, chile powder, salt and tomato sauce. When the mixture is thoroughly blended, set the sauce aside.

To serve the mixed chaat, divide the potato and chick pea mixture between 4 plates. Place the pastry squares on top. Spoon the yogurt sauce and tamarind chutney over the pastry. Garnish each plate with fresh cilantro, peanuts and a sprinkle of set, if you like. Serve the mixed chaat cold, with the Rosewater-flavored Lassi (recipe below).

Illustrated on page 14.

Rosewater-flavored Lassi, with Chopped Pistachio Nuts

Lassi is traditionally served in chaat shops in India. There are many different lassi recipes, some sweet and some salty. This one, flavored with saffron or rosewater and sprinkled with chopped, unsalted, raw pistachios, is absolutely sumptuous!

1¼ CUPS PLAIN YOGURT

2½ CUPS WATER

2–3 TABLESPOONS SUGAR

1 TEASPOON ROSEWATER, OR TO TASTE

2 TEASPOONS CHOPPED, FRESH PISTACHIO NUTS

(OPTIONAL)

Place the yogurt in a jug and whisk with a wire whisk for about 2 minutes. Pour in the water, sugar and rosewater. Continue to whisk for a further 3–5 minutes.

Serve chilled, sprinkled with chopped pistachios, if you like.

VARIATION
Saffron-flavored Lassi
Instead of the rosewater, substitute 1 pinch of saffron threads, steeped for about 30 minutes in water. Continue as in the main recipe, and serve with or without the pistachio nuts.

Curry Puffs with Vegetable Pastry

Curry Puffs can be served hot as an appetizer or at a drinks party. They are also suitable for a light lunch when served with a salad – and, when cold, absolutely ideal for taking on picnics, or as a packed lunch.

1 POTATO, DICED

½ CAULIFLOWER, CUT INTO FLOWERETS

⅓ CUP FROZEN PEAS

⅓ CUP GREEN BEANS, SLICED

2 TABLESPOONS TOMATO PASTE

1 TABLESPOON LEMON JUICE

1 TEASPOON GARLIC PULP

1 TEASPOON GINGER PULP

1½ TEASPOONS CHILE POWDER

1 TEASPOON GROUND CORIANDER

1 TEASPOON GARAM MASALA

1 TEASPOON SALT

4 TABLESPOONS CORN OIL

½ TEASPOON WHITE CUMIN SEEDS

1 ONION, DICED

⅔ CUP WATER

6 TABLESPOONS HEAVY CREAM

1 TABLESPOON CHOPPED FRESH CILANTRO

1 EGG, WHISKED

ROUGH PUFF PASTRY

2¼ CUPS ALL-PURPOSE FLOUR

½ TEASPOON SALT

¾ CUP (1½ STICKS) BUTTER

⅔ CUP WATER

Put all the prepared vegetables in a bowl, cover with water and set aside.

Meanwhile, mix the tomato paste, lemon juice, garlic, ginger, chile powder, ground coriander, garam masala and salt in a small bowl.

Heat the oil in a heavy-bottom saucepan and sauté the white cumin seeds and onion until golden brown. Lower the heat, stir in the tomato paste mixture and stir-fry for about 3 minutes.

Drain the potato, cauliflower, peas and beans and add to the saucepan. Stir well. Pour in the measured water, cover and cook for about 3–5 minutes, until the vegetables are cooked. Remove the lid and continue cooking, stirring, until the liquid has been fully absorbed, then pour in the cream and add the fresh cilantro.

Cook for a further 3–5 minutes, so that the sauce thickens. Set the sauce aside to cool and make the rough puff pastry.

For the pastry, sift the flour and salt into a large mixing bowl. Cut the butter into small cubes and drop these onto the flour, covering them fully with flour. Begin to stir the measured water in gradually, mixing to form a soft dough.

Set the dough aside in a cool place for about 15 minutes.

Roll out the pastry on a lightly floured board. Fold the pastry into half, roll out again and repeat this process again so you end up with 2–3 layers.

Start to break off small balls (about 4-6 depending on the size of the curry puffs you want) and roll these out into rounds about 4–5 inches across. Put tablespoonfuls of the vegetable curry mixture on one half of each round. Dampen the edges slightly with water and fold over into pasty shapes. Brush with the whisked egg. When all the pastries are ready, put on an ovenproof dish and bake in a preheated moderate oven, 350°F, for about 15–20 minutes.

Spicy Mushroom and Fresh Cilantro Soup

Cilantro is an annual herb, now widely available in supermarkets. However, if you like growing your own herbs, it will be happy in the garden, or in a pot on the windowsill. It originated in Europe, where it was a favorite in Ancient Rome, and migrated eastward to India and southeast Asia, and it is a particular favorite in Thailand.

6 TABLESPOONS (¾ STICK) BUTTER

½ BUNCH SCALLIONS, CHOPPED

3 CUPS MUSHROOMS

2 TABLESPOONS FRESH CILANTRO

½ TEASPOON SALT

½ TEASPOON CHILE POWDER

½ TEASPOON GARLIC POWDER

2 TABLESPOONS LEMON JUICE

1¼ CUPS WATER

1¼ CUPS LIGHT CREAM

TO GARNISH

FEW SPRIGS FRESH CILANTRO

1 TABLESPOON CREAM

½ SMALL SCALLION, FINELY CHOPPED

Melt the butter in a saucepan over low heat. Add the chopped scallions and cook them for 2 minutes before adding the mushrooms, cilantro, salt, chile powder, garlic powder and lemon juice.

Continue to stir-fry for about 3 minutes, then pour in the water and cream. Stir the mixture gently, taste and adjust the seasoning, if necessary.

Transfer the mixture to a food processor and blend until smooth, about 1 minute. Return the soup to the saucepan and bring to a boil.

Transfer to 4 individual serving bowls and serve, garnished with the cilantro, cream and the scallion.

Spicy Vegetarian Croquettes

These vegetable croquettes are very delicious! Try varying the vegetables you choose to put in them. Other root vegetables could be used, in season.

2 LARGE POTATOES, BOILED AND COARSELY MASHED

1 SMALL CARROT, BOILED AND DICED

¼ CUP PEAS, BOILED

¼ CUP CANNED CORN

2 FRESH GREEN CHILES, CHOPPED

1 TABLESPOON CHOPPED FRESH CILANTRO

2 TEASPOONS MANGO POWDER

1 TEASPOON SALT

APPROX 1¼ CUPS CORN OIL

4 CURRY LEAVES

½ TEASPOON ONION SEEDS

½ TEASPOON MUSTARD SEEDS

2 EGGS, BEATEN

1½ CUPS BREAD CRUMBS

TO GARNISH

½ ICEBERG LETTUCE, SHREDDED

1 ONION, SLICED IN RINGS

1 TOMATO, SLICED

1 LIME, CUT IN WEDGES

In a large bowl, mix together the mashed potatoes, diced carrot, peas, corn, chopped chiles, fresh cilantro, mango powder and salt.

Heat 1 tablespoon of oil in a saucepan until hot. Lower the heat to medium and add the curry leaves, onion seeds and mustard seeds, letting them sizzle for 1 minute. Remove the saucepan from the heat, add the vegetable mixture, mixing thoroughly and set aside to cool.

When the mixture is cool, make about 12 croquettes. Dip them into the beaten eggs and then roll them in the bread crumbs, coating them thoroughly. Set aside.

Heat the remaining oil in a karahi or deep skillet and cook the croquettes in batches, using a slotted spoon to turn them frequently, until golden brown.

Remove from the pan with a slotted spoon and drain on absorbent paper towels.

Serve the croquettes garnished with iceberg lettuce, onion slices, tomato slices and lime wedges.

Vegetable Pakoras

Pakoras are small pieces of vegetable, which are dipped in a marvellously light batter, made from besun or gram flour, then deep-fried. This is a delicious, simple dish – serve it as an appetizer accompanied by chutneys or dipping sauces, as finger-food with drinks, or as a side dish with other curry dishes.

4 TABLESPOONS GRAM FLOUR

2 TABLESPOONS ALL-PURPOSE FLOUR

1½ TEASPOONS SALT

1 TEASPOON BAKING SODA

1½ TEASPOONS CRUSHED DRIED RED CHILES

1 TEASPOON CRUSHED CORIANDER SEEDS

1 TEASPOON CRUSHED POMEGRANATE SEEDS

1 TEASPOON CRUSHED WHITE CUMIN SEEDS

¼ TEASPOON TURMERIC

3 TABLESPOONS CHOPPED FRESH CILANTRO

3–4 GREEN CHILES, CHOPPED

1¼ CUPS WATER

1 ONION, SLICED

1 LARGE POTATO, CUT INTO STRIPS

8–10 FRESH SPINACH LEAVES

½ SMALL CAULIFLOWER, CUT INTO FLOWERETS

OIL FOR DEEP-FRYING

Sift the gram flour, all-purpose flour, salt and baking soda into a bowl. Add spices, chopped cilantro and green chiles to the bowl, then gradually pour in the water, mixing it in with a fork to form a smooth batter.

Add the prepared vegetables to the batter. If it feels too stiff, pour in a little water to loosen the mixture.

Heat the oil in a karahi or deep skillet and drop in about 1 tablespoon of batter at a time and deep-fry, turning once, over a medium heat.

Remove each pakora with a slotted spoon once it is cooked and drain on absorbent paper towels. Repeat the process until all the batter is finished. This amount of mixture should make about 12–15 pakoras.

Serve the vegetable pakoras immediately with a spicy tomato sauce or tamarind chutney.

RIGHT: *Two excellent recipes to serve as appetizers – at the top, Vegetable Pakoras (recipe above, right) and below, Spicy Vegetarian Croquettes (recipe above). Both are equally good to serve at a drinks party, together with Spicy Tomato Ketchup or Spicy Dip on page 117 or one of the Tamarind Chutneys on page 111.*

Panir and Vegetable Samosas

These samosas make an excellent snack any time of day and can also be served as an appetizer with any of the chutneys in this book.

2 POTATOES, COARSELY DICED

1 CARROT, COARSELY DICED

1¼ CUPS CORN OIL

1 SMALL ONION

¼ TEASPOON ONION SEEDS

¼ CUP FROZEN CORN

¼ CUP FROZEN PEAS

½ CUP PANIR (SEE PAGE 67), CUT INTO SMALL CUBES

1 TABLESPOON FINELY CHOPPED FRESH CILANTRO

2 RED CHILES, CHOPPED

1 TEASPOON CHILE POWDER

1 TEASPOON MANGO POWDER

½ TEASPOON SALT

PASTRY

1½ CUPS SELF-RISING FLOUR

½ TEASPOON SALT

4 TABLESPOONS (½ STICK) BUTTER, CUT INTO SMALL CUBES

6 TABLESPOONS WATER

Cook the potatoes and carrots in boiling salted water until cooked but not mushy. Drain and set aside.

Heat 3 tablespoons of oil in a heavy-bottom saucepan until hot and sauté the onion and onion seeds for 2 minutes. Lower the heat, add the potatoes, carrots, corn and peas and lightly sauté them for about 1 minute before adding the panir cubes, cilantro, chopped chiles, chile powder, mango powder and salt. Mix gently, remove the pan from the heat and let cool.

Meanwhile, make the pastry. Sift the flour and salt into a bowl. Add the butter and rub into the flour using your fingertips until the mixture resembles bread crumbs. Pour in the water gradually, mixing it in with a fork. Pat the dough into a ball and knead with the back of your hand for 5 minutes or until the dough is smooth. Dust the dough with a little flour, cover and set aside.

Break the dough into 5–6 balls and roll out very thinly into circles. Cut in half, dampen the edges of each semi-circle and shape them into cones. Fill the cones with a little of the cooled vegetable filling, dampen the top and bottom of the edges and pinch together to seal. Set aside.

Heat the remaining oil in a karahi or deep skillet until hot. Carefully lower the samosas into the oil a few at a time and cook for 2–3 minutes or until golden brown, turning them over at least once.

Remove the samosas from the oil with a slotted spoon and drain on paper towels. They are best served immediately, but may be reheated in a moderate oven or a microwave.

Spicy Diamond-shaped Pastry Bites
(Namak Paras)

These are a delicious snack – very easy to make, and much, much more delicious than potato chips. They are very good as nibbles at a drinks party too. Although it is not traditional, you could serve them with a dip, such as a dhaal from the Beans, Peas and Lentils chapter. Also suitable would be one of the chutneys or pickles from the Accompaniments chapter. Many of these Indian snacks can be very spicy. If you find yourself "overheated," never drink water or alcohol to cool the fires – it simply doesn't work. Instead, try yogurt, bananas or coconut. Yogurt is cooling in dips, or in the traditional drink, lassi.

1½ CUPS SELF-RISING FLOUR

1 TEASPOON SALT

4 TABLESPOONS (½ STICK) UNSALTED BUTTER, CUT INTO SMALL CUBES

½ TEASPOON CRUSHED DRIED RED CHILES

½ TEASPOON WHITE CUMIN SEEDS

WATER

Sift the flour and salt into a mixing bowl. Add the butter, chiles and cumin seeds. Using your hands, blend together, gradually pouring in sufficient water to form a soft dough.

Dust the dough with flour and knead it for 3–5 minutes. Let the dough rest for 10–15 minutes.

Break the dough into two pieces and roll each piece out on a lightly floured surface to a thickness of about ⅛-inch. Using a very sharp knife, cut the dough into 2-inch diamond shapes.

Heat the oil in a karahi or deep skillet to 350°F, or until a cube of bread browns in 30 seconds, and cook the pastry diamonds in batches, turning them once, until golden. Remove them from the pan with a slotted spoon and drain on absorbent paper towels.

Uppuma

Indian cooking is unbeatable for its huge range of snacks and savories. Many of these are perfect for serving at cocktail parties, although these parties were not, until recently, part of the largely teetotal Indian way of life. A stroll down any Indian street will often produce an enormous variety of different foods available from street stalls. These range from delicious drinks of freshly-squeezed sugar-cane juice to dozens of bite-size treats such as those described in this chapter. Semolina flour is used to make various sweet dishes, and also this recipe for uppuma, which can be served as a savory snack any time of day. Semolina is the hard part of the wheat grain, and is used to make couscous in North Africa, and pasta and puddings in western cooking.

2 TABLESPOONS CHANA DHAAL
3 TABLESPOONS CORN OIL
1 TEASPOON MUSTARD SEEDS
8–10 CURRY LEAVES
1 TABLESPOON PEANUTS
1 TABLESPOON CASHEW NUTS
1½ TEASPOONS SALT
½ CUP PEAS
1½ CUPS COARSE SEMOLINA FLOUR
½ TEASPOON DRIED RED CHILES, CRUSHED
2½ CUPS WATER
2 TABLESPOONS LEMON JUICE

Wash the chana dhaal, boil it until soft, drain and set aside.

Heat the oil in a large skillet until hot and sauté the mustard seeds and curry leaves for a few seconds.

Lower the heat and add the peanuts and cashew nuts, cooking them quickly before adding salt, peas, semolina flour, red chiles and the chana dhaal and stir-fry for about 1 minute.

Pour in the water and cook for about 3 minutes or until the water is fully absorbed.

Pour in lemon juice and serve.

VARIATION
Uppuma with Urid Dhaal and Fresh Cilantro
You could also substitute whole black urid dhaal for the chana dhaal, and add about 1 tablespoon chopped, fresh cilantro leaves to the mixture before stir-frying.

Sautéed Spicy Peas

Ideal to serve with cocktails. The only problem is that these spicy peas disappear at an unbelievable rate, so for a large party I suggest you make multiple quantities. I find that frozen peas are not only easier to deal with, but their quality is more dependable.

1 LB FROZEN PEAS, THAWED
1¼ CUPS OIL
1 TEASPOON CHILE POWDER
½ TEASPOON GROUND CORIANDER
1 TEASPOON SALT
1 TEASPOON MANGO POWDER

Put the peas in a strainer to drain off any excess liquid.

Heat the oil in a heavy-bottom saucepan or karahi and sauté the peas for 3–5 minutes. Remove from the pan with a slotted spoon and drain on absorbent paper towels.

Meanwhile, in a large mixing bowl, mix together the chile powder, ground coriander, salt and mango powder. Put the peas in the bowl, hold a large plate on top and shake thoroughly so the peas are well coated with the spices.

Stir-fried Cauliflower and Peas

A quick and easy dish to prepare, which can be served as a side dish with any lentil dish.

4 TABLESPOONS CORN OIL
1 ONION
½ TEASPOON BLACK CUMIN SEEDS
3 BLACK CARDAMOMS
6 BLACK PEPPERCORNS
1-INCH PIECE CINNAMON STICK
1 TEASPOON SALT
¼ TEASPOON TURMERIC
2 RED CHILES, SLICED
1 SMALL CAULIFLOWER, BROKEN INTO FLOWERETS
1½ CUPS PEAS
2 TABLESPOONS CHOPPED FRESH CILANTRO
1 TABLESPOON LEMON JUICE

Heat the oil in a wide pan to 350°F, or until a cube of bread browns in 30 seconds, and sauté the onion with the cumin seeds, cardamoms, black peppercorns and cinnamon for about 2 minutes. Stir in salt, turmeric, red chiles, cauliflower flowerets and peas and continue to stir-fry for a further 5 minutes. Finally, add the cilantro and lemon juice and serve.

Curries

Many of your vegetarian meals may be planned around splendidly varied, deliciously spicy recipes in this chapter. There is a very wide choice of curries, from simple combinations of one or two lightly spiced vegetables, suitable for an everyday family meal, to more elaborate dishes suitable for an elegant dinner party.

Doodhi or Marrow with Moong Dhaal

(Kaddu Aur Moong Dhaal)

This curry goes particularly well with chapatis, and marries doodhi with its "soul mate," fenugreek.

1 BUNCH FRESH FENUGREEK

5 TABLESPOONS CORN OIL

2 ONIONS, DICED

½ TEASPOON MIXED FENUGREEK SEEDS AND

ONION SEEDS

1 TEASPOON GROUND CUMIN

1 TEASPOON GARLIC PULP

¼ TEASPOON TURMERIC

1 TEASPOON CHILE POWDER

1½ LB DOODHI, OR MARROW, CUT INTO 1-INCH CUBES

1 TEASPOON SALT

¼ CUP MOONG DHAAL,

WASHED AND DRAINED

1 TABLESPOON LEMON JUICE

Prepare the fenugreek by breaking off the leaves.

Heat the oil in a karahi or deep skillet, add the onions, fenugreek seeds and onion seeds and sauté until golden brown. Lower the heat and add the ground cumin, garlic, turmeric, chile powder, fenugreek leaves and doodhi or marrow cubes and stir-fry for about 3 minutes.

Add the salt, then the moong dhaal and lemon juice. Cover the pan and cook for 5–7 minutes over a very low heat, stirring occasionally, until the dhaal is cooked and the doodhi is soft.

VARIATIONS

Chayote with Moong Dhaal

Chayote, sometimes known as "choko," is sold in Caribbean markets as "chow-chow." This small, pale green vegetable is also a variety of marrow and grows on a climbing vine. It is suitable for recipe, as well as the one on the rught, with fenugreek. Peel a similar quantity of chayotes and chop into 1-inch cubes – you don't have to remove the seeds; they have a lovely, nutty taste. Proceed as in the main recipe.

PREVIOUS PAGES: *From left, Stir-fried Baby Onions with Panir (recipe page 67) and Cauliflower in a Hot and Sour Sauce (recipe page 59). Panir is a very versatile Indian cheese, either crumbly like cottage cheese, or firm like soft cheddar. It can be cut into cubes, fried in ghee, and added to many dishes such as this one with baby onions.*

Doodhi or Marrow with Fenugreek

(Kaddu Aur Methi)

Doodhi is an Indian variety of marrow, also known as squash, and is available in Asian specialty stores. Ordinary marrows or large zucchinis are a perfect substitute, and you will find that these methods of preparation make the rather bland flavor of marrow really come into its own. Baby patty-pan squash in green or yellow may also be used. Doodhi and fragrant fenugreek go very well together. In this recipe, stir-frying brings out the flavor of the fenugreek.

4 TABLESPOONS CORN OIL

½ TEASPOON MIXED WHITE CUMIN SEEDS

AND FENUGREEK SEEDS

2 ONIONS, SLICED

¼ TEASPOON TURMERIC

1 TEASPOON CHILE POWDER

1 TEASPOON SALT

1½ LB DOODHI OR MARROW,

CUT INTO 1-INCH CUBES

1 BUNCH FRESH FENUGREEK LEAVES

2 GREEN CHILES, CHOPPED

1 X 1-INCH PIECE FRESH GINGER, SHREDDED

Heat the oil in a saucepan, add the cumin and fenugreek seeds and stir-fry for about 1 minute, then add the sliced onions and continue cooking for about 3 minutes. Lower the heat and stir in the turmeric, chile powder and the salt.

Next add the doodhi or marrow pieces, fresh fenugreek leaves, and green chiles. Using a wooden spoon, stir-fry for about 2 minutes, then lower the heat further, cover the saucepan and cook for 5–7 minutes. Remove the lid and add the shredded ginger. Cook for a further 2 minutes.

Serve hot with puris.

VARIATIONS

Pumpkin with Fenugreek

Pumpkin is from the same botanical family as marrow, and can be happily adapted to this recipe. Substitute a similar quantity of peeled, deseeded and cubed pumpkin, and add 1 teaspoon of nutmeg at the same time as the chile powder. Pumpkin and nutmeg have a special affinity for each other.

Zucchini with Fenugreek

Slice 1½ lb zucchini into 1-inch pieces and proceed as in the main recipe. Do not peel the zucchini.

Vegetables Cooked with Bulgar Wheat

(Subzee Ka Haleem)

This is a recipe from the north of India – the wheat-growing region of the country. Bulgar wheat is also known as "cracked wheat," and is available either roasted or plain. It is a popular ingredient in vegetarian cooking, in some homemade mueslis, and is the major component of the Lebanese salad, tabbouleh.

1 CUP BULGAR (CRACKED) WHEAT

6 TABLESPOONS CORN OIL

2 ONIONS, DICED

½ TEASPOON BLACK CUMIN SEEDS

3 WHOLE GREEN CARDAMOMS

1 TEASPOON GARAM MASALA

1½ TEASPOONS GROUND CORIANDER

1½ TEASPOONS CHILE POWDER

1 TEASPOON GARLIC PULP

1 TEASPOON GINGER PULP

1½ TEASPOONS SALT

¼ TEASPOON TURMERIC

1 X 1-INCH PIECE CINNAMON STICK

2 POTATOES, DICED

1 EGGPLANT, DICED

2 TOMATOES, SLICED

1 BUNCH FRESH FENUGREEK LEAVES

1 SMALL CAULIFLOWER, BROKEN INTO FLOWERETS

¾ CUP PLAIN YOGURT

3 GREEN CHILES, CHOPPED

2 TABLESPOONS CHOPPED FRESH CILANTRO

3 TABLESPOONS LEMON JUICE

TO GARNISH

4 TABLESPOONS CLARIFIED BUTTER

1 ONION, SLICED

2 X 1-INCH PIECES FRESH GINGER, SHREDDED

2 GREEN CHILES, CHOPPED

1 TABLESPOON CHOPPED FRESH CILANTRO

1 TABLESPOON CHOPPED FRESH MINT

1 LIME, CUT INTO WEDGES

Soak the cracked wheat in water, preferably overnight.

Heat the oil in a heavy-bottom saucepan, add the onions and sauté until golden brown. Lower the heat and add all the spices, stirring continuously.

Next, add the prepared potatoes, eggplant, tomatoes, fenugreek leaves and cauliflower, mix together gently and stir-fry continuously for about 2 minutes.

Beat the yogurt and pour into the pan, then add the chopped chiles, fresh cilantro and lemon juice. Lower the heat further,

cover the saucepan and cook for 5–7 minutes, stirring occasionally to prevent the vegetables sticking.

Drain the cracked wheat and add it to the vegetables in the saucepan, mixing it in thoroughly.

If the mixture (called a *haleem*) seems too thick, add about ⅔ cup water to loosen the consistency.

Cook for about 1 minute, remove the pan from the heat and transfer to a serving dish. Keep the *haleem* warm while you prepare the garnish.

Heat the clarified butter in a skillet and sauté the sliced onion until crisp and golden brown. While it is still hot and sizzling, pour it over the top of the *haleem* and garnish with the shredded ginger, green chiles, fresh cilantro and mint. Serve with lime wedges and the naan bread recipe below.

Naan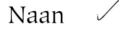

Most Indian breads, such as those found on pages 102–103, are unleavened. Naan is the exception, widely used with curries in order to mop up the delicious sauces. In India, it is also used as an eating utensil, to pick up pieces of food, rather like an edible spoon or pair of tongs. Naan would be most often served in the north of the country, where breads are the basis of most meals. In the south, rice is the staple food, and a meal would be unthinkable without it. Naan is usually cooked in a tandoor oven, which produces a fierce heat. It would be impossible to replicate that heat in an ordinary domestic oven, and this recipe uses the broiler instead. There are many naan bread recipes, but this one is easy to follow.

1 TEASPOON SUGAR

1 TEASPOON FRESH YEAST

⅔ CUP WARM WATER

2 CUPS ALL-PURPOSE FLOUR

1 TABLESPOON CLARIFIED BUTTER

1 TEASPOON SALT

4 TABLESPOONS (½ STICK) UNSALTED BUTTER

1 TEASPOON POPPY SEEDS

Dissolve the sugar and yeast in a cup with the warm water, then set aside for 10 minutes or until the mixture is frothy.

Place the flour in a large mixing bowl, make a well in the center, add clarified butter, salt and yeast mixture. Mix well with your fingers, adding more water if required.

Knead on a floured surface for about 5 minutes or until smooth. Place the dough back in the bowl, cover and leave to rise in a warm place for 1½ hours or until doubled in size. Turn onto a floured surface and knead for a further 2 minutes.

Break off small balls and pat into rounds about 5 inches in diameter and ½-inch thick. Place on a greased sheet of tinfoil and place under a very hot broiler for 7–10 minutes, turning twice to brush with butter and sprinkle with poppy seeds. Serve immediately or wrap in tinfoil until required.

Tomato Kadi
(Tamatar Ki Kadi)

Kadi, a dish from South India, is probably also the word from which "curry" is derived.

¾ CUP RED TAMARIND PASTE

1¼ CUPS WATER

3 TABLESPOONS CORN OIL

1 ONION, DICED

1 TEASPOON GINGER PULP

1 TEASPOON GARLIC PULP

1 TEASPOON GROUND CUMIN

¼ TEASPOON TURMERIC

1 TEASPOON CHILE POWDER

1 TEASPOON SALT

1 TEASPOON GROUND CORIANDER

3 TOMATOES, QUARTERED

3 TABLESPOONS GROUND RICE

2 TABLESPOONS CHOPPED FRESH CILANTRO

FOR THE BAGHAAR TARICA

3 TABLESPOONS OIL

½ TEASPOON WHITE CUMIN SEEDS

3 DRIED RED CHILES

6 CURRY LEAVES

TO GARNISH

FRESH CILANTRO

GREEN CHILES

Soak the tamarind paste in hot water to cover for about 15–20 minutes. Squeeze the softened tamarind with your hand to extract as much pulp as possible and push it through a strainer. Pour the measured water onto the pulp to loosen it and then set aside.

Meanwhile, heat the oil in a saucepan over a medium heat and sauté the onion until golden brown. Lower the heat and gradually stir in the ginger, garlic, cumin, turmeric, chile powder, salt, ground coriander and the tamarind pulp. Increase the heat, add the tomatoes and bring to a boil. Then lower the heat and slowly stir in the ground rice, a little at a time, stirring continuously. Add the fresh cilantro and cook slowly for 3–5 minutes. Remove the pan from the heat and set aside.

Prepare the baghaar tarica; heat the oil in a skillet and sauté the cumin seeds, red chiles and curry leaves until they turn a shade darker. Pour over the kadi while still sizzling.

Serve garnished with fresh cilantro and green chiles.

Vegetable Jalfrezi
(Subzee Ki Jalfrezi)

Though panir is not generally used in this hot and spicy dish, I find that it enhances the flavor of the curry – and, of course, panir is a very good source of protein.

5 TABLESPOONS CORN OIL

½ TEASPOON MIXED ONION SEEDS, MUSTARD SEEDS AND FENUGREEK SEEDS

4 CURRY LEAVES

3 TABLESPOONS TOMATO PASTE

1 TEASPOON GROUND CUMIN

1½ TEASPOONS GROUND CORIANDER

1 TEASPOON GINGER PULP

1 TEASPOON GARLIC PULP

1 TEASPOON CHILE POWDER

2 TEASPOONS SALT

2 TEASPOONS MANGO POWDER

1¼ CUPS WATER

VEGETABLES

3 TOMATOES, CUT INTO WEDGES

½ SWEET GREEN PEPPER, DESEEDED AND SLICED

½ SWEET RED PEPPER, DESEEDED AND SLICED

1 LARGE CARROT

⅔ CUP GREEN BEANS

½ CUP PANIR

2 GREEN CHILES, DESEEDED AND SLICED

2 TABLESPOONS FRESH CILANTRO

⅔ CUP WATER

Heat the oil in a heavy-bottom saucepan, add all the whole seeds and curry leaves and sauté them until they change color. Remove the pan from the heat and set aside.

Mix the tomato paste, all the spices and water together and pour into the saucepan containing the oil, seeds and curry leaves. Return to the heat and cook for about 2 minutes.

Gradually add the vegetables, panir and the green chiles to the pan, stirring to coat with the spiced oil.

Add the fresh cilantro and water, cover the pan and cook over a very low heat until all the vegetables are cooked.

Serve the curry hot with rice or chapatis.

RIGHT: *From top: Tomato Kadi (recipe above) and Vegetable Jalfrezi (recipe above, left).*

Vegetables in a Tangy Sauce
(Khutti Meethi Subzee)

This sauce is packed with flavor – feel free to substitute other vegetables in season for the ones listed here. Cauliflowers, zucchini and marrow would also be delicious in this recipe.

⅓ CUP TOOR DHAAL

1¼ CUPS WATER

2 TABLESPOONS GREEK YOGURT

1 TABLESPOON TOMATO PASTE

2 TEASPOONS RED TAMARIND PASTE

⅔ CUP WATER

1 TEASPOON GINGER PULP

1 TEASPOON GARLIC PULP

1½ TEASPOONS CHILE POWDER

½ TEASPOON SUGAR

1 TEASPOON SALT

1 TEASPOON GROUND CUMIN

1 TEASPOON GROUND CORIANDER

3 TABLESPOONS CORN OIL

4 WHOLE CURRY LEAVES

½ TEASPOON ONION SEEDS

4 WHOLE DRIED RED CHILES

½ TEASPOON WHITE CUMIN SEEDS

12–14 BABY ONIONS

12 BABY POTATOES, HALVED AND BOILED

12–14 CHERRY TOMATOES

2 CARROTS, THICKLY SLICED

⅓ CUP LIGHT CREAM

2 TABLESPOONS CHOPPED FRESH CILANTRO

3 GREEN CHILES

Boil the toor dhaal in the 1¼ cups water until soft but not mushy and set aside.

Mix together the yogurt, tomato paste, tamarind paste, the water, ginger, garlic, chile powder, sugar, salt, cumin and ground coriander together in bowl and set aside.

Heat the oil in a karahi or deep skillet, add the curry leaves, onion seeds, dried red chiles and cumin seeds and sauté over a medium heat until they are a shade darker. Add the whole baby onions and stir-fry them until they are browned all over. Add the baby potatoes, cherry tomatoes and carrots, and stir-fry continuously. Pour in the yogurt mixture and cook for 2 minutes, then stir in the cream.

Finally, mix in the fresh cilantro and green chiles and serve the vegetables hot.

Illustrated on page 95.

Vegetables in a Rich Creamy Sauce

⅔ CUP GREEK YOGURT

1 TABLESPOON TOMATO PASTE

2 TABLESPOONS LEMON JUICE

1 TEASPOON GINGER PULP

1 TEASPOON GARLIC PULP

1 TEASPOON CHILE POWDER

1 TEASPOON SALT

1 TEASPOON GROUND CORIANDER

1 TEASPOON GROUND CUMIN

2 TABLESPOONS GROUND ALMONDS

⅔ CUP WATER

⅓ CUP (¾ STICK) UNSALTED BUTTER

4 TABLESPOONS CORN OIL

½ TEASPOON MIXED ONION SEEDS AND MUSTARD SEEDS

6 SMALL THICK GREEN CHILES, SLIT DOWN THE CENTER AND DESEEDED

8–10 CAULIFLOWER FLOWERETS

4–5 BABY POTATOES, THICKLY SLICED

1 CARROT, SLICED

5 BABY ONIONS

8–10 PANIR CUBES

1¼ CUPS WATER

¾ CUP LIGHT CREAM

2 TABLESPOONS CHOPPED FRESH CILANTRO

2 GREEN CHILES, CHOPPED

½ CUP FLAKED ALMONDS, TO GARNISH

Blend the yogurt, tomato paste, lemon juice, ginger, garlic, chile powder, salt, ground coriander, cumin, ground almonds and water in a mixing bowl and set aside.

Heat the unsalted butter and oil in a karahi or deep skillet. Add the onion and mustard seeds and sauté until they turn a shade darker. Sauté the vegetables, one kind at a time, in the oil until they are cooked, starting with the green chiles then the cauliflower, potatoes, carrot, and whole baby onions, and ending with the panir cubes. Remove the cooked vegetables from the pan, with a slotted spoon and drain on paper towels.

Add the spice and yogurt mixture to the remaining butter and oil in the pan. Pour in the measured water and cook for about 5 minutes, until the sauce comes to a boil. Return the cooked vegetables to the pan, stirring gently to mix the vegetables and sauce together, without breaking them.

Finally, pour in the cream, fresh cilantro and green chiles and cook for 3–5 minutes.

Serve garnished with the flaked almonds.

Cauliflower in a Creamy Sauce

Cauliflower seems to be particularly suited to creamy sauces, but you could also substitute other vegetables in this curry.

1 TEASPOON GROUND CORIANDER

2 TEASPOONS GROUND ALMONDS

2 ONIONS, COARSELY CHOPPED

1 TEASPOON GARLIC PULP

1 TEASPOON GINGER PULP

1 TEASPOON SALT

3 GREEN CHILES, CHOPPED

2 TABLESPOONS CHOPPED FRESH CILANTRO

1 TABLESPOON CORN OIL

⅓ CUP (¾ STICK) BUTTER

4 CURRY LEAVES

½ CAULIFLOWER, CUT INTO SMALL FLOWERETS

½ SWEET GREEN PEPPER, DESEEDED AND DICED

½ SWEET RED PEPPER, DESEEDED AND DICED

⅔ CUP HEAVY CREAM

Blend the ground coriander, ground almonds, onions, garlic, ginger, salt, 2 of the green chiles and 1 tablespoon of the cilantro in a food processor for 1 minute or until the mixture is fairly smooth.

Heat the oil and butter together in a heavy-bottom saucepan, add the curry leaves and sauté until they are a shade darker.

Pour the spice and onion mixture into the pan and stir-fry over a medium heat for about 3 minutes, or until the onion mixture is cooked.

Add the cauliflower flowerets and continue to stir-fry the contents of the pan for a further 2 minutes.

Then add the green and red peppers, the cream and the remaining cilantro and green chile. Cook through for 2 minutes and serve hot with puris. (See recipe on page 102.)

Shahi Panir Koftas

This curry has a delicious and creamy sauce. Served with freshly made masala puri, (see recipe on page 102) it makes an excellent meal. Panir, which is a very good source of protein, is eaten all over India. Though panir is available in Asian specialty stores, the homemade variety is best for this recipe. There is another recipe for preparing panir on page 67.

PANIR

5 CUPS WHOLE MILK

2 TABLESPOONS LEMON JUICE

SHAHI PANIR KOFTA SAUCE

⅓ CUP (¾ STICK) BUTTER

1 TABLESPOON CORN OIL

1 CINNAMON STICK

2 GREEN CARDAMOMS

3 TABLESPOONS PLAIN YOGURT

3 TABLESPOONS TOMATO PASTE

1 TEASPOON GARAM MASALA

1 TEASPOON CHILE POWDER

¼ TEASPOON TURMERIC

1 TEASPOON GROUND CORIANDER

1 TEASPOON SALT

1 TABLESPOON LEMON JUICE

⅔ CUP WATER

2 TABLESPOONS CHOPPED FRESH CILANTRO

2 GREEN CHILES, CHOPPED

1 CUP LIGHT CREAM

First, make the panir. Bring the milk slowly to a boil over a medium heat then add the lemon juice, stirring continuously. The milk will now begin to thicken and curdle. Wait until all the liquid (the whey) has evaporated and you are left with the curdled milk (the curds).

Strain the curdled milk through a strainer and press down to get rid of any excess liquid. When cool, divide the mixture into 8–10 spoonfuls and mold them into small balls, a little smaller than a golf ball, making sure they look smooth. Set the panir balls aside on a plate in the refrigerator.

For the sauce, heat the butter and oil in a medium-size saucepan. When the butter has melted, add the cinnamon stick and the cardamoms and sauté for a few seconds. Remove the pan from the heat and set aside.

Mix together the yogurt, tomato paste, garam masala, chile powder, turmeric, ground coriander, salt, lemon juice and water together in bowl.

Return the saucepan to the heat, pour in the yogurt mixture and cook over a medium to low heat. Drop the koftas into the sauce, followed by the fresh cilantro, chiles and cream and mix gently together, stirring continuously. Cook for a further 5 minutes, or until the sauce has thickened.

Mixed Vegetables in a Butter Sauce

(Mili Huwi Subzee Makhan Ki Sauce May)

This is sure to be a favorite with your family and friends. It has a rich sauce and is full of flavor.

⅓ CUP GREEK YOGURT

1 TABLESPOON TOMATO PASTE

½ TEASPOON GARAM MASALA

1 TEASPOON GINGER PULP

1 TEASPOON CHILE POWDER

¼ TEASPOON GROUND CARDAMOMS

1 TEASPOON GARLIC PULP

1 TEASPOON GROUND CORIANDER

1 TEASPOON SALT

¼ TEASPOON COARSELY GROUND BLACK PEPPER

⅓ CUP (¾ STICK) BUTTER

1 TABLESPOON CORN OIL

2 ONIONS, DICED

2 BAY LEAVES

2 PIECES CINNAMON BARK

2 POTATOES, COARSELY DICED

1 LARGE CARROT, SLICED

⅓ CUP GREEN BEANS, SLICED

½ CAULIFLOWER, CUT INTO SMALL FLOWERETS

2 FRESH GREEN CHILES, CHOPPED

3 TABLESPOONS CHOPPED FRESH CILANTRO

1¼ CUPS WATER

⅔ CUP LIGHT CREAM

Mix the yogurt, tomato paste, garam masala, ginger, chile powder, cardamoms, garlic pulp, ground coriander, salt and pepper in a medium-size bowl and set aside.

Heat the butter and oil in a karahi or deep skillet, add the onions, bay leaves and cinnamon bark and sauté until the onions are golden brown. Pour the yogurt and spice mixture into the pan and stir-fry for about 1 minute.

Reduce the heat to low and let the spices cook slowly while preparing the vegetables.

Gradually stir the potatoes, carrot, beans, cauliflower, green chiles and fresh cilantro into the pan. Add the water. Cook over a low heat until the vegetables are tender, but still firm enough to retain their shape and texture.

Pour in the cream and heat the dish to boiling point. Serve it with any of the rice dishes in this book.

Potatoes and Eggplants Cooked in Whole Spices

(Allo Baigun Aur Sabuth Masalay)

Potatoes were not introduced to India until the 16th century – probably by the Portuguese. Eggplants, however, are native to the sub-continent, and spread from there to almost every corner of the world. They are now particular favorites in all the countries around the Mediterranean. The two vegetables are delicious culinary partners in this dish – but it is important to choose small eggplants for this recipe.

4 TABLESPOONS CHOPPED FRESH CILANTRO

5 GREEN CHILES, CHOPPED

2 TABLESPOONS CHOPPED FRESH MINT

2 BUNCHES SCALLIONS, CHOPPED

4 TABLESPOONS CORN OIL

½ TEASPOON ONION SEEDS

4 CURRY LEAVES

4 GARLIC CLOVES

1 X 1-INCH PIECE FRESH GINGER, SHREDDED

1 TEASPOON SALT

2 POTATOES, COARSELY CUBED

4 SMALL EGGPLANTS, COARSELY CUBED

½ CUP WATER

Place 3 tablespoons of the cilantro, 3 of the green chiles, the mint and the scallions in a food processor and grind them for about 1 minute.

Heat the oil in a saucepan, add the onion seeds, curry leaves, garlic and shredded ginger and sauté for about 1 minute. Add the ground mixture from the processor to the pan, lower the heat and stir-fry for about 2 minutes. Add the potatoes and eggplants, mix together and pour in the measured water. Cover the saucepan with a tight-fitting lid and cook gently for 12–15 minutes.

When the vegetables are cooked, add the remaining cilantro and green chiles and cook, stir-frying, for a further 2 minutes before serving.

OPPOSITE: *Mixed Vegetables in a Butter Sauce (recipe above, left), served with Aromatic Rice (recipe on page 92). Both dishes would be suitable for inclusion in a thali (recipe on page 75), the traditional Indian vegetarian meal. The thali is particularly associated with the largely-vegetarian south of India, but is now found all over the sub-continent, in the simplest village home and the grandest restaurants.*

Potatoes and Green Beans in a Coconut Sauce
(Aloo Phalli)

This mild curry with a thick creamy sauce comes from the coconut-growing south of India. It is delicious served with plain boiled rice.

1 CUP PLAIN YOGURT

¼ CUP COCONUT MILK

1½ TEASPOONS GARAM MASALA

1 TEASPOON CHILE POWDER

1 TEASPOON GINGER PULP

1 TEASPOON GARLIC PULP

¼ TEASPOON TURMERIC

¼ TEASPOON BLACK CUMIN SEEDS

¼ TEASPOON GROUND CARDAMOM

1 TEASPOON SALT

4 TABLESPOONS (½ STICK) BUTTER

2 TABLESPOONS OIL

2 ONIONS, FINELY DICED

2 POTATOES, CUT IN ½-INCH DICE

⅓ CUP GREEN BEANS

½ CAULIFLOWER, CUT INTO SMALL FLOWERETS

½ SWEET RED PEPPER, DESEEDED AND DICED

1 TABLESPOON CHOPPED FRESH CILANTRO

3 TABLESPOONS CREAM

Beat the yogurt together with the coconut milk, garam masala, chile powder, ginger, garlic, turmeric, cumin seeds, cardamom and salt.

Heat the butter and oil in a heavy-bottom saucepan, add the onions and stir-fry until browned. Pour in the yogurt mixture and stir-fry, for a further 2 minutes.

Lower the heat and add the remaining ingredients. Cover the pan and cook until the vegetables are soft but not mushy.

VARIATION

Okra, Tomatoes and Potatoes in a Coconut Sauce

Substitute ½ lb fresh young okra, 3 medium-size potatoes and 2 tomatoes for the potatoes and green beans in the main recipe. Rinse the okra and pat dry. Peel the potatoes and cut into large dice.

Proceed as in the main recipe, adding the tomatoes, cut into quarters, towards the end of the cooking time.

Potatoes with Sesame Seeds
(Aloo Thill)

Sesame seeds – widely used in Indian and Chinese cooking – have a delicious, sweet, nutty flavor. Look for the unhulled seeds in shops which stock a wide variety of Asian spices, rather than the common, hulled, creamy-colored ones – you will really notice the difference in taste.

3 POTATOES, COARSELY DICED

5 TABLESPOONS OIL

1 ONION, DICED

1 TEASPOON WHITE CUMIN SEEDS

¼ TEASPOON TURMERIC

1 TEASPOON CHILE POWDER

1 X 1-INCH PIECE FRESH GINGER, SHREDDED

1 TEASPOON SALT

2 FRESH RED CHILES, CHOPPED

1 TABLESPOON CHOPPED FRESH CILANTRO

2 TABLESPOONS SESAME SEEDS

Cook the potato dice in lightly salted water until soft. Drain and set aside.

Heat the oil in a karahi or deep skillet, add the onion and cumin seeds and sauté until the onions are lightly browned.

Lower the heat, mix in the turmeric, chile powder, ginger and salt and mix in well. Add the cooked potatoes and stir-fry for about 2 minutes.

Add the red chiles, fresh cilantro and sesame seeds and stir to mix well. Serve hot with naan (see recipe on page 34) or chapatis (see recipe on page 102).

Aloo Gobi

Literally, "potatoes and cauliflower" – two favorite vegetarian ingredients. This is a dry vegetable curry which is delicious when served with any of the wet dhaal recipes on pages 76–89.

5 TABLESPOONS CORN OIL

1 TEASPOON WHITE CUMIN SEEDS

4 WHOLE DRIED RED CHILES

1 PINCH ASAFOETIDA

1 TABLESPOON SHREDDED GINGER

3 GARLIC CLOVES

2 POTATOES, COARSELY DICED

1 SMALL CAULIFLOWER, CUT INTO SMALL FLOWERETS

1 TEASPOON SALT

2 FRESH RED CHILES, CHOPPED

1 TABLESPOON CHOPPED FRESH CILANTRO

1 TABLESPOON LEMON JUICE

2 TOMATOES, QUARTERED

Heat the oil in a heavy-bottom saucepan and sauté the cumin seeds, the dried red chiles and asafoetida for a few seconds. Lower the heat and add the ginger and garlic cloves. Cook for about 20 seconds then add the potatoes and stir-fry on the lowered heat for about 3 minutes.

Next, add the cauliflower flowerets and continue to gently stir-fry for a further 2 minutes.

Stir in the salt, red chiles, cilantro, lemon juice and tomatoes. Cover the pan and cook over a very low heat for 12–15 minutes, stirring very gently occasionally to ensure even cooking. Serve the Aloo Gobi hot.

VARIATION

Pumpkin and Broccoli Curry

Pumpkin and broccoli make an interesting and colorful variation for this recipe. Just remember that pumpkin cooks much faster than potatoes and broccoli cooks faster than cauliflower. Follow the main recipe, but cook for only 8–10 minutes, or until the pumpkin is tender.

Potato and Pea Korma
(Aloo Matar Ka Korma)

Korma dishes, a legacy of the Mogul's rule in India, are very popular with Westerners who are new to very spicy food, since they are mild and creamy. So – if you are having guests who might be a little wary of very hot curry, serve korma, and they will love it! This one has a delicious and thick sauce and should be served with paratas.

2 TEASPOONS POPPY SEEDS

2 TEASPOONS SESAME SEEDS

7 TABLESPOONS PLAIN YOGURT

1 TEASPOON GARAM MASALA

1 TEASPOON GINGER PULP

1½ TEASPOONS GROUND CORIANDER

1 TEASPOON GARLIC PULP

1 TEASPOON CHILE POWDER

1 TEASPOON SALT

1 TABLESPOON LEMON JUICE

1 TABLESPOON TOMATO PASTE

5 TABLESPOONS MELTED BUTTER

1 TABLESPOON CORN OIL

2 WHOLE GREEN CARDAMOMS

4–6 BLACK PEPPERCORNS

1 X 1-INCH PIECE CINNAMON BARK, HALVED

2 ONIONS

10 BABY POTATOES

¼ CUP FROZEN GREEN BEANS

¼ CUP FROZEN PEAS

2 TOMATOES, QUARTERED

1 TEASPOON CHOPPED FRESH CILANTRO

1 TEASPOON FRESH MINT

LIGHT CREAM

First, dry-roast the poppy seeds and sesame seeds (see page 8). When cool, place the seeds in a spice grinder and grind to a powder. Remove from the grinder and place in a bowl.

Add the yogurt, garam masala, ginger, ground coriander, garlic, chile powder, salt, lemon juice and tomato paste. Using a whisk, blend together and set aside.

Heat the butter with the corn oil in a heavy-bottom saucepan and drop in the cardamoms, peppercorns and cinnamon bark. Next, add the onions and fry until they are golden brown.

Pour in the yogurt and spice mixture and stir-fry for about 2 minutes over a low heat.

Add the potatoes, beans and peas and stir.

If the mixture seems too dry, add ⅔ cup water. Cover the pan and cook until the vegetables are cooked.

Add the tomato quarters, fresh cilantro, fresh mint and stir in the cream. Cook for a further 2 minutes, then serve hot.

Onion Bhajias and Vegetables in a Yogurt and Gram Flour Sauce

(Dahl Ki Kadi)

Bhajias are a favorite Indian dish in the west. They can be served as a main dish, as here, or simply as a starter. You will find recipes for Mushroom and Leek Bhajias and plain Onion Bhajias in the Appetizers and Snacks chapter on page 21. India boasts a wide selection of snack foods, and bhajias are perhaps the most widely-known of all these.

1 CUP GRAM FLOUR

1½ TEASPOONS CHILE POWDER

1 TEASPOON SALT

½ TEASPOON BAKING SODA

1 ONION, SLICED

2 GREEN CHILES

1 TABLESPOON CHOPPED FRESH CILANTRO

⅔ CUP WATER

APPROX 1¼ CUPS CORN OIL

YOGURT GRAM FLOUR SAUCE

1¼ CUPS PLAIN YOGURT

2 TABLESPOONS GRAM FLOUR

1¼ CUPS WATER

1 TEASPOON GINGER PULP

1 TEASPOON GARLIC PULP

1 TEASPOON CHILE POWDER

1½ TEASPOONS SALT

½ TEASPOON TURMERIC

1 TEASPOON GROUND CORIANDER

1 TEASPOON GROUND CUMIN

1 ZUCCHINI, SLICED

6 SMALL CAULIFLOWER FLOWERETS

1 SMALL SWEET RED PEPPER, DESEEDED AND COARSELY DICED

2 GREEN CHILES, CHOPPED

1¼ CUPS CORN OIL

BAGHAAR TARICA

3 TABLESPOONS CORN OIL

4 CURRY LEAVES

1 TEASPOON MIXED ONION SEEDS, MUSTARD SEEDS AND WHITE CUMIN SEEDS

3 DRIED RED CHILES

2 TABLESPOONS CHOPPED FRESH CILANTRO, TO GARNISH

To make the bhajia batter, mix the gram flour, chile powder, salt, baking soda, onion slices, green chiles, fresh cilantro and water together in a medium-size bowl.

Prepare the yogurt gram flour sauce; in a large bowl, whisk the yogurt with the gram flour and water, and then add the ginger and garlic and all the spices. Pour the mixture through a strainer into a medium-size saucepan, place over a low heat and bring to a boil, stirring occasionally and adding a little extra water, if the sauce gets too thick. Gradually add the zucchini, cauliflower, red pepper and green chiles and continue to cook over a low heat until the vegetables are cooked. Transfer to a serving dish and set aside.

To make the bhajias, heat the corn oil in a karahi or a deep skillet to 350°F, or until a cube of bread browns in 30 seconds. Start sautéeing the gram flour batter, dropping about a tablespoon at a time into the hot oil and turning it at least twice. Sauté over a medium heat until they turn a golden brown. Remove the bahjias from the oil with a slotted spoon, and place them on top of the yogurt gram flour sauce.

To make the baghaar tarica, heat the oil in a small saucepan until it is quite hot and then add the curry leaves, onion seeds, mustard seeds, white cumin seeds and dried red chiles; within 30 seconds they should turn a shade darker. Remove the saucepan from the heat and pour the baghaar tarica over the bhajias and sauce.

Garnish the dish with chopped fresh cilantro and serve immediately with plain boiled rice and a pat of butter.

RIGHT: *Bhajias are one of the best-known Indian snack foods. However, this dish of Onion Bhajias and Vegetables in a Yogurt and Gram Flour Sauce (recipe above), served with plain boiled rice, makes the bhajia into a much more substantial main-course dish.*

Buttered Saag
(Makhani Saag)

Try to use fresh young spinach leaves for this recipe, as it really helps to improve the flavor. However, if this is not available, frozen leaf spinach will do. This is perhaps the simplest and easiest way to serve spinach in an Indian menu. Use good, unsalted butter, to form clarified butter, if you wish. This will stop the butter from burning quite so easily. To clarify butter, place it in a saucepan and bring it to a boil. It will separate into golden butter and whitish milk solids. Pour off the clarified butter, leaving the milk solids behind.

2 LB YOUNG SPINACH LEAVES

⅔ CUP BUTTER

1 LARGE ONION, DICED

1 X 1-INCH PIECE FRESH GINGER, SHREDDED

3 GARLIC CLOVES, SLICED

¼ TEASPOON TURMERIC

1 TEASPOON CHILE POWDER

1 TEASPOON GARAM MASALA

1 BUNCH FRESH CILANTRO, CHOPPED

2 TABLESPOONS LEMON JUICE

TO GARNISH

2 RED CHILES, SLICED

1 X1-INCH PIECE FRESH GINGER, SHREDDED

1 TOMATO, DESEEDED AND DICED

¼ CUP (½ STICK) PAT OF BUTTER

Wash the spinach leaves thoroughly and coarsely chop. Cook the spinach in the water left on the leaves until soft. Drain, squeeze out any excess water and set aside.

Melt the butter in a karahi or deep skillet over a medium heat and gently sauté the onion until soft with the ginger, garlic, turmeric, chile powder and garam masala. Add the spinach and stir-fry for about 5 minutes.

Add the fresh cilantro and mix it into the spinach, stirring continuously over a low heat. Then pour in the lemon juice. Transfer to a warmed serving dish and serve garnished with the red chiles, ginger, diced tomato and pat of butter.

Saag with Toor Dhaal

Saag, or spinach, is cooked with tomatoes in many different cuisines. Certainly their flavors go well together, but perhaps it's their colors which are so attractive. The red and green is repeated in the garnish of red chiles and fresh green cilantro.
This dish may also be made using chana dhaal, instead of the toor dhaal.

1 LB FRESH SPINACH LEAVES, BLANCHED

AND COARSELY CHOPPED

¼ CUP TOOR DHAAL

4 TABLESPOONS CORN OIL

14 OUNCE CAN TOMATOES

1 TEASPOON GINGER PULP

1 TEASPOON GARLIC PULP

1½ TEASPOONS GROUND CORIANDER

1 TEASPOON GROUND CUMIN

1 TEASPOON CHILE POWDER

2 TABLESPOONS LEMON JUICE

2 RED CHILES, CHOPPED

2 TABLESPOONS CHOPPED FRESH CILANTRO

Blanch the spinach in boiling water for about 3 minutes. Drain and squeeze out any excess liquid and set aside.

Wash the toor dhaal and cook in lightly salted boiling water until soft but not mushy. Drain and set aside.

Heat the oil in a karahi or a deep skillet over a low heat and while it is heating mix the tomatoes and their juice, ginger, garlic, ground coriander, ground cumin, chile powder and lemon juice together in a bowl. Pour the mixture into the oil and sauté for at least 5–7 minutes.

Once the sauce has thickened add the spinach and cook, stirring occasionally, for 5–7 minutes.

Pour in the toor dhaal, the red chiles and fresh cilantro.
Serve hot with rice or chapatis.

Methi and Spinach Panir

Fenugreek is known as "methi" in India. It is available in Asian specialty stores, but is not difficulty to grow it yourself. It is a plant which originated in the Middle East, and is used in cooking there, in North Africa and India. The leaves have a very strong scent, and are used either fresh (as here), or dried, as a vegetable or herb. The seeds are also used – they are slightly bitter until roasted or cooked gently in hot oil. They smell rather like celery. Panir, the delicious Indian cooking cheese, can be bought at specialist shops, or you can make it yourself from the recipe on page 67.

¾ CUP PANIR

5 TABLESPOONS CORN OIL

¼ CUP (½ STICK) BUTTER

1 POTATO, CUT INTO FRENCH FRIES

LARGE BUNCH OF FRESH FENUGREEK LEAVES

½ LB FROZEN SPINACH

1 TEASPOON GINGER PULP

1 TEASPOON SALT

1 TEASPOON GROUND CORIANDER

¼ TEASPOON TURMERIC

1 TEASPOON CHILE POWDER

2 TABLESPOONS CHOPPED FRESH CILANTRO

2 RED CHILES, CHOPPED

⅓ CUP PLAIN YOGURT

½ CUP CORN

Cut the panir into cubes. Heat the oil and the butter in a heavy-bottom saucepan or a skillet with a lid, add the panir cubes and sauté until they are slightly golden. Remove them from the pan with a slotted spoon and drain on paper towels. Set aside.

Add the potato french friess to the saucepan and sauté until they are lightly golden. Remove from the oil and set aside on paper towels to drain.

Wash and drain the fenugreek leaves and spinach to the pan and sauté for about 2 minutes before adding the ginger, salt, ground coriander, turmeric, chile powder and fresh cilantro. Reduce the heat and continue to stir-fry for about 3 minutes until all the spices are cooked.

Add the red chiles and stir in the yogurt and corn.

Continue to stir-fry gently until the yogurt has been absorbed into the spinach.

Finally, add the panir cubes and potatoes. Cover and cook for 5-7 minutes. Serve hot with boiled rice.

Tinday Methi with Moong Dhaal

Tinday is a vegetable very similar to doodhi (kaddu) in texture and flavor – and you could also substitute squash, marrow or even zucchini. If you are unable to find the fresh vegetable, canned tinday are widely available in Asian specialty shops, and are equally good. If you are using canned tinday, drain off the liquid first.

1 BUNCH FRESH FENUGREEK LEAVES

3 TABLESPOONS MOONG DHAAL, WASHED

5 TABLESPOONS CORN OIL

2 ONIONS, FINELY DICED

¼ TEASPOON ONION SEEDS

4–6 CURRY LEAVES

3 TOMATOES, DICED

1 TEASPOON GINGER PULP

1 TEASPOON GARLIC PULP

1½ TEASPOONS CHILE POWDER

¼ TEASPOON GROUND FENNEL

1 TEASPOON SALT

1 LB TINDAY, DICED

⅔ CUP WATER (SEE METHOD)

3 GREEN CHILES, CHOPPED

Wash the fenugreek leaves and set aside.

Cook the moong dhaal in lightly salted boiling water until it is soft. Drain and set aside.

Heat the oil in a heavy-bottom saucepan, add the onions, onions seeds and curry leaves and stir-fry until the onions are golden brown. Add the diced tomatoes and cook for 2 minutes. Lower the heat.

Next, add the ginger, garlic, chile powder, ground fennel and salt and continue to stir-fry for a further 1 minute.

Stir in the fresh fenugreek leaves and continue to stir-fry, until the fenugreek is a shade darker.

Add the tinday and, if necessary, pour in the water. Cover the pan and cook until the tinday is soft and almost mushy.

Add the moong dhaal and green chiles. Cook for 1 more minute, transfer to a heated serving dish and serve while hot.

Stuffed Sweet Green and Red Peppers

(Bharay Huway Simla Mirch)

Sweet peppers, like their close cousins, chiles, are now so common in Indian cooking that it's easy to forget that they were only introduced to the region in the 16th century. They were probably first brought to Goa by the Portuguese, and spread through the rest of the country from there.

2 POTATOES

2 SWEET GREEN PEPPERS, HALVED AND DESEEDED

2 SWEET RED PEPPERS, HALVED AND DESEEDED

3 TABLESPOONS CORN OIL

½ TEASPOON ONION SEEDS

1 LARGE ONION, DICED

1 SMALL CAULIFLOWER, CUT INTO SMALL FLOWERETS

1 CARROT, DICED

⅓ CUP CORN

1 TEASPOON GINGER, SHREDDED

1½ TEASPOONS GROUND CORIANDER

1 TEASPOON GARLIC PULP

1 TEASPOON CHILE POWDER

1 TABLESPOON TOMATO PASTE

1 TABLESPOON LEMON JUICE

TO GARNISH

FRESH CILANTRO SPRIGS

CHOPPED GREEN CHILES

Cook the potatoes in boiling salted water. Once they are cooked, drain, then mash them down coarsely and set aside. Put the prepared peppers in an ovenproof dish.

Heat the oil in a deep skillet and sauté the onion seeds for about 20 seconds. Add the onion and continue sautéeing until golden brown. Next, add the cauliflower flowerets, diced carrots, corn and mashed potatoes, then add the ginger, ground coriander, garlic, chile powder, tomato paste and lemon juice. Continue to stir-fry over a low heat for 3–5 minutes, cool the mixture slightly then use to stuff the peppers. Garnish with the fresh cilantro and chopped green chiles.

Pour about 1 tablespoon of oil over the peppers to prevent them sticking and bake in a preheated moderate oven, 350°F, for about 10–12 minutes.

LEFT: *From top, Stuffed Green and Red Peppers (recipe above) and Marrow Koftas in a Creamy Sauce (recipe above, right).*

Marrow Koftas in a Creamy Sauce

1–1½ LB MARROW

2 TABLESPOONS ALL-PURPOSE FLOUR

2 TABLESPOONS GRAM FLOUR

1 TEASPOON CHILE POWDER

1½ TEASPOONS GROUND CORIANDER

1 TEASPOON GARAM MASALA

1 TEASPOON SALT

¼ TEASPOON TURMERIC

1 TABLESPOON FRESH CILANTRO LEAVES

6 TABLESPOONS CORN OIL

CREAMY SAUCE

2 ONIONS, CHOPPED

2 TABLESPOONS TOMATO PASTE

1 TEASPOON GARLIC PULP

1 TEASPOON GROUND CUMIN

1½ TEASPOONS GROUND CORIANDER

2 GREEN CHILES, CHOPPED

2 TEASPOONS COCONUT POWDER

1 TABLESPOON FRESH MINT

1 TABLESPOON FRESH CILANTRO

1 TEASPOON SALT

1 TABLESPOON PLAIN YOGURT

5 TABLESPOONS CORN OIL

2 TOMATOES, CUT INTO QUARTERS

½ CUP CREAM

Peel, deseed and coarsely chop the marrow and boil until it is soft and mushy. Drain and squeeze out any excess moisture.

Mix the all-purpose flour, gram flour, chile powder, ground coriander, garam masala, salt, turmeric and cilantro together in a bowl and add to the marrow. Blend together and form the mixture into small balls, about the size of a golf ball.

Heat the oil in a karahi or deep skillet and gently sauté the koftas gently, moving them around in the oil so that they brown all over. Remove from the pan and set aside.

For the sauce, place the onions, tomato paste, garlic, ground cumin, ground coriander, green chiles, coconut powder, mint, fresh cilantro, salt and yogurt in a food processor and blend together for about 1 minute, stopping once to stir the mixture with a spatula. Transfer to a bowl and set aside.

Heat the corn oil in a heavy-bottom saucepan until very hot and reduce the heat to medium before adding the onion and spice mixture. Cook, stirring occasionally to prevent it from catching at the bottom of the pan, for 5–7 minutes, lowering the heat, if necessary. Add the tomatoes, pour in the cream and stir to mix.

Gently drop the koftas into the sauce one by one. Partly cover the saucepan with a lid and cook over a low heat for about 3–5 minutes. Serve hot with rice.

Panir with Mushrooms in a Creamy Sauce

Mushrooms are not very widely used in India, but all Indian cooks enthusiastically adopt whatever interesting vegetables are to hand. It was in the north-west frontier state of Kashmir where mushrooms were most common in traditional cooking. Nowadays, they are often used by Indians living in other parts of the world. There are now a number of different kinds of mushrooms available, and I would use white, brown cap or chestnut mushrooms in this recipe. The rather subtle flavor of oyster mushrooms would, I think, be somewhat overwhelmed by the spices in this dish. Panir can be bought at specialist shops, or you can make your own from the recipe on page 67.

½ CUP (1 STICK) BUTTER

1 TABLESPOON CORN OIL

1 BAY LEAF

2 ONIONS, FINELY DICED

⅔ CUP WATER

1 TEASPOON GARLIC PULP

1 TEASPOON GINGER PULP

1 TEASPOON GROUND CUMIN

1 TEASPOON GROUND CORIANDER

1 TEASPOON CHILE POWDER

¼ TEASPOON TURMERIC

1 TABLESPOON SALT

⅔ CUP BROCCOLI, CUT INTO TINY FLOWERETS

¾ CUP MUSHROOMS, SLICED

⅔ CUP PANIR, CUT INTO CUBES

¾ CUP LIGHT CREAM

1 TABLESPOON CHOPPED FRESH CILANTRO

2 RED CHILES, SLICED

Melt the butter with the corn oil in a heavy-bottom saucepan and sauté the bay leaf and the onions until golden brown. Pour in the water, lower the heat, cover and cook for 3–5 minutes.

Meanwhile, mix together the garlic, ginger, ground cumin, ground coriander, chile powder, turmeric and salt in a small bowl. Pour the mixture over the onions, which should now be cooked and fairly dry. Stir-fry for about 1 minute.

Add the broccoli, mushrooms and panir and blend together.

Stir in the cream, then the cilantro and chiles. Cook for about 2 minutes, transfer to a serving dish and serve with rice.

Mushrooms in a Creamy Fennel Sauce

Fennel is not much used in India as a vegetable. In fact, the Florence fennel variety, with its thick bulbous base, is not much grown there. The variety used in India is grown for its seeds, which are a common ingredient in many spice mixtures. They have a distinctive aniseed taste, and just a single teaspoon of them in this recipe will give a delightfully fresh taste to the whole dish. Again, use ordinary white cultivated mushrooms, or the chestnut or brown cap mushrooms which I think seem to have a little more flavor than the common white variety.

6 TABLESPOONS (¾ STICK) BUTTER

1 TABLESPOON OIL

2 ONIONS, DICED

1 TEASPOON FENNEL SEEDS

1 BAY LEAF

1 TEASPOON GINGER PULP

1 TEASPOON GARLIC PULP

¼ TEASPOON TURMERIC, CRUSHED

1 TEASPOON BLACK PEPPERCORNS, CRUSHED

1 TEASPOON GROUND CORIANDER

3 GREEN CHILES, CHOPPED

2 CUPS MUSHROOMS

1 TEASPOON SALT

¾ CUP LIGHT CREAM

2 TABLESPOONS CHOPPED FRESH CILANTRO

½ LARGE SWEET RED PEPPER, DESEEDED AND SLICED

Heat the butter and oil in a karahi or deep skillet, over a medium heat. Add the onions, fennel seeds and the bay leaf and sauté for 3–5 minutes.

Meanwhile, blend the ginger, garlic, turmeric, black pepper and ground coriander together in a small bowl. Stir the mixture into the onions and lower the heat.

Add the green chiles, mushrooms and salt and continue to stir-fry for a further 2 minutes.

Pour in the cream, then the fresh cilantro, stirring the mixture with a wooden spoon.

Finally, add the sliced red pepper and serve.

Spicy Okra
(Masala Bhindi)

A delicious array of spices is used in this dish – their aroma will be enhanced by the first sautéeing in hot oil. Turmeric, the spice that gives this dish its color, is sometimes used instead of saffron, but it should be prized for its own qualities. When adding this spice, don't be tempted to increase the quantity in the belief that "more is better" – it can be bitter if you use too much. The best turmeric is a good, deep orange, with a lovely musky taste. Be careful, because tumeric is a very powerful dye, and if you get it on your clothes it will be just about impossible to get out.

2 ONIONS, DICED
1 TEASPOON GINGER PULP
1 TEASPOON GARLIC PULP
¼ TEASPOON TURMERIC
1 TABLESPOON COCONUT POWDER
1 TABLESPOON SESAME SEEDS
1 TEASPOON SALT
1 TEASPOON GROUND CORIANDER
1 TEASPOON CHILE POWDER
6 TABLESPOONS CORN OIL
½ TEASPOON MIXED FENUGREEK SEEDS,
ONION SEEDS AND MUSTARD SEEDS
3 CURRY LEAVES
3 TABLESPOONS OIL
1 LB OKRA, TRIMMED AND CUT INTO 1-INCH PIECES
2 RED CHILES, SLIT AND DESEEDED

Place the onions, ginger, garlic, turmeric, coconut powder, sesame seeds, salt, ground coriander and chile powder in a food processor and blend to a pulp.

Heat 3 tablespoons of the oil in a medium-size saucepan, add the seeds and curry leaves and sauté for about 30 seconds. Stir in the onion and spice mixture and cook over a medium heat, stirring occasionally.

Heat the remaining oil in a deep skillet, add the okra and lightly sauté the pieces for about 2 minutes.

With a slotted spoon, remove the okra from the pan and add to the onions. Cook for a further 3–5 minutes before adding the red chiles. Serve with paratas (see page 103).

Sautéed Okra with Panir
(Thali Huwi Bhindi Aur Panir)

Okra is widely used in Caribbean and American Creole cooking, and also in Africa and Asia. You should be able to buy okra in supermarkets, as well as from Asian specialty stores. When choosing it, make sure it is firm and fresh, with no soft spots. Check that the stalk end has not withered – a sure sign that it is past its best. Panir can also be bought at Asian specialty stores, or made at home, using the recipe on page 67.

7 TABLESPOONS CORN OIL
10 OUNCES OKRA, TRIMMED AND CUT INTO 1-INCH PIECES
¾ CUP PANIR, CUT INTO CUBES
2 ONIONS, DICED
1 TEASPOON ONION SEEDS
4 CURRY LEAVES
1 TEASPOON SALT
1 TEASPOON CHILE POWDER
1½ TEASPOONS GROUND CORIANDER
1 TEASPOON GINGER PULP
1 TEASPOON GARLIC PULP
2 TOMATOES, SLICED
1 TABLESPOON LEMON JUICE
1 TABLESPOON CHOPPED FRESH CILANTRO

Heat the oil in a karahi or deep skillet, add the okra and sauté until cooked – about 3–5 minutes. With a slotted spoon, remove the okra from the pan and drain on paper towels. Add the panir cubes to the pan and sauté in the same way. With a slotted spoon, remove the panir from the pan and drain on paper towels.

Add the onions, onion seeds and curry leaves to the oil left in the pan and sauté for about 5 minutes. Lower the heat and stir in the salt, chile powder, ground coriander, ginger and garlic. Add the tomatoes, then return the okra and panir cubes to the pan, stirring gently to coat the vegetables in the spicy oil.

Sprinkle on the lemon juice and cilantro.

Heat through and transfer the okra and panir to a serving dish. Serve hot with rice or chapatis.

VARIATION
Sautéed Okra with Panir and Peas
A delicious addition to this recipe – cook about ¾ cup of frozen peas for 2–3 minutes, then add them to the other ingredients at the same time as the tomatoes.

Okra Stuffed with Coconut
(Bhindi Aur Narial)

This is a wonderful way to cook okra – which can be rather glutinous in some dishes. They are a very attractive shape, and take very well to simple stuffings. Try them also with the even spicier variation below. When preparing okra for this dish it is very important to dry them thoroughly after washing them, and before slitting them down the middle.

1 LB OKRA

1½ TEASPOONS MANGO POWDER

3 TABLESPOONS DESICCATED COCONUT

1½ TEASPOONS GROUND CORIANDER

1 TEASPOON BROWN SUGAR

½ TEASPOON CRUSHED DRIED RED CHILES

1 TABLESPOON CHOPPED FRESH CILANTRO

4 TABLESPOONS CORN OIL

¼ TEASPOON ONION SEEDS

1 TABLESPOONS LEMON JUICE

Wash the okra and dry on absorbent paper towels. Slit each one down the middle, leaving the ends intact and set aside.

In a separate bowl, blend the mango powder, shredded coconut, ground coriander, brown sugar, crushed red chiles and fresh cilantro. Using a teaspoon, stuff each okra with as much of the spice mixture as possible.

Heat the oil in a skillet with a lid, and sauté the onion seeds. Lower the heat, lift the okra a few at a time and place them in the oil. When all the okra are in the skillet, sprinkle any remaining spice mixture on top and pour the lemon juice over. Cover the pan and cook over a gentle heat for about 10–15 minutes, checking occasionally.

Serve with puris.

VARIATION
Okra Stuffed with Chiles and Sesame Seeds
Replace the stuffing ingredients above with 2 red or green fresh chiles, finely diced, mixed with 1 tablespoon sesame seeds. Stuff the okra, then proceed as in the main recipe.

RIGHT: From top, the deliciously spicy Okra Stuffed with Coconut (recipe above) and Stuffed Baby Eggplants (recipe above, right). Okra and eggplants are two well-traveled ingredients. Eggplants were native to India, but have found their way all over the world, and are especially popular in countries north, south and east of the Mediterranean. Okra probably originated in Africa or Asia, and is now well known as a major ingredient of the American Creole dish, Gumbo.

Stuffed Baby Eggplants
(Bharay Huway Basun)

Eggplants are now available in many shapes, sizes and colors. My greengrocer has small round white ones (which justify their alternative name of "eggplant"), larger, pear-shaped purple ones, and long, curved, purple striped ones. They are perfect for stuffing.

6 BABY EGGPLANTS

5 TABLESPOONS SESAME SEEDS

7 TABLESPOONS CORN OIL

2 ONIONS, DICED

1½ TEASPOONS GROUND CUMIN

1½ TEASPOONS GROUND CORIANDER

1 TEASPOON CHILE POWDER

1 TEASPOON SALT

1 TABLESPOON LEMON JUICE

1 TABLESPOON FRESH CILANTRO

2 POTATOES, COARSELY DICED

4 TOMATOES, COARSELY DICED

½ TEASPOON MIXED FENUGREEK SEEDS, ONION SEEDS AND MUSTARD SEEDS

4–6 CURRY LEAVES

FRESH CILANTRO SPRIGS, TO GARNISH

Wash the eggplants and cut in half from the bottom end, leaving the stalk intact. Remove the soft flesh from the inside, leaving a thick shell. Set the eggplants aside.

Grind the sesame seeds to a rough texture.

Heat 4 tablespoons of the oil in a saucepan and sauté the onions until golden brown. Add the ground cumin, ground coriander, chile powder, salt, lemon juice, cilantro and potatoes and stir-fry for about 3 minutes over a medium heat.

Add the tomatoes and ground sesame seeds and continue to stir-sauté for 3–5 minutes.

Lower the heat, cover the pan and continue cooking until the potatoes are cooked. Remove the lid and continue cooking until the mixture is quite dry. Remove the pan from the heat and set aside to cool.

Stuff the eggplants with the cooled mixture.

Heat the remaining oil in a saucepan, add the whole mixed seeds and the curry leaves and sauté for a few seconds. Lower the heat, add the eggplants gently one by one, cover the pan and continue cooking for about 15 minutes, or until the eggplants are soft but not mushy.

Serve, garnished with sprigs of fresh cilantro.

Potatoes and Eggplants in Tamarind

(Aloo Baigun in Imli)

Tamarinds, known in India as "imli," are the seed pods of a tree which grows all over South-east Asia, the Caribbean and tropical Africa. They are about the size of a garden pea pod, curved, with a lovely velvety brown coat. They have a sweet-and-sour flesh, which is used in many dishes, rather as you would use lemon juice in western cooking.

5 TABLESPOONS CORN OIL

½ TEASPOON MIXED ONION SEEDS,

MUSTARD SEEDS AND FENUGREEK SEEDS

2 ONIONS, SLICED

1 TEASPOON GINGER PULP

1½ TEASPOONS GROUND CORIANDER

1 TEASPOON GARLIC PULP

¼ TEASPOON TURMERIC

1 TEASPOON CHILE POWDER

1 TABLESPOON TOMATO PASTE

1 TABLESPOON TAMARIND PASTE

⅔ CUP WATER

2 TABLESPOONS SUGAR

1 TEASPOON SALT

2 POTATOES, DICED

1 EGGPLANT, DICED

2 TOMATOES, QUARTERED

2 GREEN CHILES, CHOPPED

2 TABLESPOONS CHOPPED FRESH CILANTRO

Heat the oil in a heavy-bottom saucepan and add the onion seeds, mustard seeds and fenugreek seeds. Sauté for about 20 seconds then add the onions, continuing to stir-fry until the onions are golden brown. Lower the heat and add the ginger, ground coriander, garlic, turmeric, chile powder, tomato paste, tamarind paste, water, sugar and salt. Stir to mix.

Cover the saucepan and gently cook until the onions have softened and the sauce is thick.

Add the potatoes and eggplants, cover the pan again and cook, stirring occasionally, until the potatoes and eggplant are cooked. Stir in the tomatoes, green chiles and fresh cilantro, transfer to a warmed serving dish and serve hot.

Eggplants and Potatoes

(Aloo Baigun)

These two vegetables go very well together. In European cooking, eggplants are usually salted first to remove the dark and bitter juices. However, boiling or steaming seems to remove those juices, and eggplants are delectable in this recipe.

5 TABLESPOONS CORN OIL

2 ONIONS, FINELY DICED

1 TABLESPOON TOMATO PASTE

1½ TEASPOONS GROUND CORIANDER

1 TEASPOON GINGER PULP

1 TEASPOON GARLIC PULP

1½ TEASPOONS CHILE POWDER

1 TEASPOON SALT

¼ TEASPOON TURMERIC

1¼ CUPS WATER

2 POTATOES, DICED

1 EGGPLANT, DICED

2 TOMATOES, QUARTERED

2 TABLESPOONS LEMON JUICE

2 TABLESPOONS CHOPPED FRESH CILANTRO

Heat the oil in a heavy-bottom saucepan, add the onions and sauté for about 5 minutes. While the onions are cooking, mix the tomato paste, ground coriander, ginger, garlic, chile powder, salt and turmeric in a small bowl.

Once the onions are cooked, pour the spice mixture into the saucepan, lowering the heat at the same time. Stir-fry for about 1 minute before stirring in the water. Cover the saucepan and cook over a low heat until the onions are soft and the sauce has thickened.

Add all the vegetables, cover the saucepan again and let the vegetables cook in the steam for about 5 minutes. Check the pan after 5 minutes or so, and if the the contents seem too dry add ⅔ cup of water. Cook for a further 10 minutes.

Stir in the lemon juice and fresh cilantro and serve hot with chapatis or rice.

Mooli Curry
(Mooli Ki Bhujia)

You may have tried mooli (also known as "daikon" or Japanese radish) before in salads, such as the one on page 111 of this book. However, if you haven't cooked it before, this is a good recipe to try. In Indian stores, it is usually sold with its leaves attached, and both root and leaves may be used in the curry. If you prefer a milder curry, omit the ginger pulp and decrease the quantity of chiles.

1 LB MOOLI, COARSELY CHOPPED

¼ CUP YELLOW MOONG DHAAL

2½ CUPS WATER

1 TABLESPOON CHOPPED FRESH CILANTRO

1 TEASPOON GARLIC PULP

3 TABLESPOONS CORN OIL

2 GARLIC CLOVES

1 X 1-INCH PIECE FRESH GINGER, SHREDDED

2 BUNCHES SCALLIONS, COARSELY CHOPPED

1 TEASPOON SALT

1 TEASPOON CRUSHED DRIED RED CHILES

2 GREEN CHILES, CHOPPED

Place the mooli, moong dhaal, water, fresh cilantro, garlic and ginger pulp in a saucepan and bring to a boil. Cook until the mooli is soft enough to be squeezed by hand. Drain and squeeze out any excess water from the mooli and dhaal. Set aside.

Heat the oil in a heavy-bottom saucepan.

Add the garlic cloves and shredded ginger and sauté for a few seconds, then add the scallions, salt, crushed red chiles and green chiles.

Add the mooli and stir to mix, then continue to cook, stirring, over a low heat, for 3–5 minutes.

Serve the mooli curry hot with freshly made chapatis.

Fenugreek with Sesame Seeds
(Methi Ki Bhaaji Aut Thill)

A wonderful dish, using some of my favorite herbs and spices. If you find it difficult to buy fresh fenugreek, do try to grow it in your garden – it will repay the effort. When using fresh fenugreek always break the leaves off the stalks, as the flower and stalk can sometimes be bitter. Fenugreek's botanical name is "Trigonella foenum-graecum," which means "Greek hay." The Romans used it widely, and imported it from Greece, hence its Latin name. The Egyptians, too, used it as a vegetable, and held it in such high regard that they used its seeds when embalming the Pharaohs. It is rarely used outside India nowadays, but the seeds form a very important ingredient in spice mixtures and also in western ready-made curry powders.

2 BUNCHES FENUGREEK LEAVES

6 TABLESPOONS CORN OIL

¼ TEASPOON ONION SEEDS

3 ONIONS, SLICED

2 TEASPOONS MANGO POWDER

1 TEASPOON GINGER PULP

1 TEASPOON GARLIC PULP

1 TEASPOON CHILE POWDER

1 TEASPOON GROUND CORIANDER

⅔ CUP WATER

2 TOMATOES, DICED

3 TABLESPOONS SESAME SEEDS

1 TABLESPOON CHOPPED FRESH CILANTRO

Break the fenugreek leaves from the stalks and wash them thoroughly. Drain and set aside.

Heat the oil in a heavy-bottom saucepan and sauté the onion seeds and onions over a medium heat until they are soft and golden brown.

Lower the heat and add all the spices. Continue to stir-fry for about 2 minutes, then add the fenugreek leaves, and the water. Cover the pan and cook for 5–7 minutes.

Remove the lid from the saucepan and stir-fry until you begin to see some free oil on the sides of the pan.

Add the diced tomatoes, sesame seeds and chopped fresh cilantro and gently mix together. Transfer to a warmed serving dish to serve.

Fresh Stir-fried Spinach with Coconut
(Thaazi Saag Aur Narial)

Saag, or spinach, is one of the most popular vegetables in Indian cooking. It is an all-purpose word for any number of leafy green vegetables, which vary according to the season and the region.

3 TABLESPOONS MASOOR DHAAL

1½ LB FRESH SPINACH

2 ONIONS, COARSELY CHOPPED

1 RED CHILE, CHOPPED

1 TEASPOON GINGER PULP

1 TEASPOON GARLIC PULP

1 TEASPOON SALT

1 TEASPOON CHILE POWDER

3 TABLESPOONS LEMON JUICE

1 TEASPOON BROWN SUGAR

7 TABLESPOONS CORN OIL

1 TABLESPOON CHOPPED FRESH CILANTRO

2 TABLESPOONS SHREDDED COCONUT

Boil the masoor dhaal until soft, drain off all the water and then set aside.

Wash the spinach thoroughly, chop coarsely and place in a saucepan with the water left on the leaves. bring to a boil, drain thoroughly and set aside.

Place the onions, red chile, ginger, garlic, salt, chile powder, lemon juice and brown sugar in a food processor and grind for about 20–30 seconds until blended together.

Heat the oil in a saucepan, pour in the onion and spice mixture and stir-fry over a low heat for 3–5 minutes. Add the spinach, masoor dhaal, fresh cilantro and half the shredded coconut and continue to stir-fry for a further 3–5 minutes.

Transfer the spinach to a warmed serving dish, sprinkle over the remaining coconut and serve.

RIGHT: *Fresh Stir-fried Spinach with Coconut (recipe above) and Masala Vegetables (recipe above, right). Spinach is known as "saag" in India – an all-purpose word which covers many green leafy vegetables. You could substitute similar ingredients, such as Swiss chard, beet tops or spring greens. The Masala Vegetable recipe could, similarly, be adapted to other vegetables in season.*

Masala Vegetables

"Masala" simply means a mixture of spices, and that mixture can vary according to its region of origin, the ingredients it is to accompany, and also the spices the cook has on the shelf at the moment. "Garam masala" means "hot spices," and is used in the cooking of North India. Garam masala contains cardamom seeds, nutmeg, cinnamon and mace – all spices popular in the cooler north. You can buy it ready-made or prepare it yourself by grinding its component spices together. There are mixtures that are used for other purposes, such as a tandoori masala, and other mixtures from the various regions of India. Southern masalas are fiery hot, and in Goa the mixtures often contain tamarind.

3 TABLESPOONS COCONUT POWDER

2 TEASPOONS GROUND CORIANDER

1 TEASPOON CHILE POWDER

½ TEASPOON CRUSHED BLACK PEPPERCORNS

1 TEASPOON GARAM MASALA

1 TEASPOON GARLIC PULP

1 TEASPOON GINGER PULP

¼ TEASPOON TURMERIC

1 TABLESPOON TAMARIND PASTE

1 TEASPOON SALT

1 TEASPOON POPPY SEEDS

⅔ CUP WATER

5 TABLESPOONS CORN OIL

2 ONIONS, FINELY CHOPPED

1 SMALL CAULIFLOWER, BROKEN INTO SMALL FLOWERETS

1 LARGE CARROT, DICED

2 POTATOES, DICED

⅓ CUP FROZEN PEAS

⅓ CUP CORN

1 TABLESPOON CHOPPED FRESH CILANTRO

2 RED CHILES

2 TEASPOONS SOFT BROWN SUGAR

In a bowl, mix the coconut powder together with the ground coriander, chile powder, black pepper, garam masala, garlic, ginger, turmeric, tamarind, salt and poppy seeds. Stir in the water to form a paste.

Heat the oil in a heavy-bottom saucepan, add the onions and sauté until golden brown. Pour the spice mixture into the onions and stir-fry over a low heat for 2–3 minutes.

Start to add the vegetables one by one, stirring all the time. Finally, add the fresh cilantro, red chiles and brown sugar.

Cover the pan and steam cook the vegetables over a very low heat until they are all cooked. If the dish seems too dry to cook the vegetables by steaming, just add ⅔ cup water to the pan.

Serve with rice or chapatis.

Deep-fried Vegetables in Yogurt Sauce
(Thali Huwi Subzee Dhahee May)

Indian cooks don't use a great deal of oil when deep-frying, because they only cook a few items at a time. Here, each of the vegetables is deep-fried separately before being added to the yogurt mixture. The spices are then cooked in another small pan before being sprinkled over the other ingredients.

2 CUPS PLAIN YOGURT

1 TABLESPOON FINELY CHOPPED FRESH MINT

1 TABLESPOON FINELY CHOPPED FRESH CILANTRO

1 TEASPOON SALT

1 TEASPOON SUGAR

2 GREEN CHILES, FINELY CHOPPED

⅔ CUP WATER

1¼ CUPS CORN OIL

2 MEDIUM POTATOES, DICED

¾ CUP GREEN BEANS

¾ CUP CORN

1 CARROT, SLICED

½ CAULIFLOWER, CUT INTO FLOWERETS

2 TABLESPOONS CORN OIL

½ TEASPOON WHITE CUMIN SEEDS

½ TEASPOON ONION SEEDS

½ TEASPOON MUSTARD SEEDS

½ TEASPOON FENUGREEK SEEDS

6 CURRY LEAVES

½ TEASPOON GROUND CUMIN

½ TEASPOON GROUND CORIANDER

½ TEASPOON CHILE POWDER

1 TABLESPOON CHOPPED FRESH CILANTRO

Beat the yogurt in a large serving bowl and add the mint, cilantro, salt, sugar, chiles and water. Beat for a further minute and set aside.

Heat the oil in a karahi or deep skillet to 375°F, or until a cube of bread browns in 30 seconds, add the potatoes and sauté in batches until cooked. With a slotted spoon, remove from the pan and drain on absorbent paper towels. Repeat the deep-frying process with all the vegetables. Add them to the yogurt mixture.

Heat the 2 tablespoons oil in a skillet and sauté all the seeds and the curry leaves for about 30 seconds. Pour the sizzling oil and seeds over the vegetables in yogurt.

Sprinkle the ground cumin, coriander and chile powder over the yogurt and serve garnished with the cilantro.

Stuffed Chiles
(Bhari Huwi Subzee)

Try to choose thick green and red chiles for this recipe, as they are easier to seed and stuff than the thin chiles. Remember that the hottest parts of any chile are the seeds and membranes, so be sure to remove them. Remember also not to touch your face or eyes with your fingers when you have been handling chiles – the juice is just as fiery as the vegetable itself.

¾ CUP PANIR

½ TEASPOON GARAM MASALA

½ TEASPOON SALT

1 TEASPOON MANGO POWDER

12 GREEN CHILES

12 RED CHILES

3 TABLESPOONS CORN OIL

1 TEASPOON MIXED ONION SEEDS, MUSTARD SEEDS, WHITE CUMIN SEEDS AND FENUGREEK SEEDS

1 TEASPOON CRUSHED DRIED RED CHILES

1 TABLESPOON LEMON JUICE

Cut the panir into thin strips to fit into the chiles.

Mix the garam masala, salt and mango powder together and pour the mixture onto the panir strips.

Cut both the red and green chiles in half horizontally, while keeping them intact at the top, and remove the seeds. Fill the chiles with the spicy panir.

Heat the oil in a karahi or deep skillet, add all the seeds and crushed red chiles and sauté for about 1 minute.

Gently drop in the stuffed chiles and sauté them for about 2–3 minutes, moving them carefully in the pan to ensure that the filling does not fall out.

Transfer the stuffed chiles to a warmed serving dish and sprinkle the lemon juice on top. Serve while hot.

Cauliflower in a Hot and Sour Sauce

Another recipe using the lemony flavor of tamarind – the "hot" provided by the spices, and the "sour" by the tamarind.

6 OUNCES RED TAMARIND PASTE

1¼ CUPS HOT WATER

4–5 TABLESPOONS CORN OIL

1 TEASPOON MIXED ONION SEEDS,
MUSTARD SEEDS AND FENUGREEK SEEDS

5 CURRY LEAVES

2 ONIONS, DICED

½ TEASPOON TURMERIC

1 TEASPOON GROUND CUMIN

1½ TEASPOONS GROUND CORIANDER

1 TEASPOON GINGER PULP

½ TEASPOON GARLIC PULP

1 TEASPOON CHILE POWDER

1¼ CUPS WATER

1 TEASPOON SALT

1 CAULIFLOWER, CUT INTO FLOWERETS

4 RED CHILES, SLICED

2 TABLESPOONS CHOPPED FRESH CILANTRO

Break the tamarind paste down and soak it in the hot water for at least 15 minutes. Squeeze the water from the tamarind and push the tamarind pulp through a strainer. Once all the pulp has been extracted, set aside in a bowl.

Meanwhile, heat the oil in a heavy-bottom saucepan, add the mixed seeds, curry leaves and onions and stir-fry for about 3 minutes. Add the turmeric, ground cumin, ground coriander, ginger, garlic, chile powder, water and salt and cook for about 5–7 minutes. Add the tamarind pulp, cauliflower flowerets, red chiles and fresh cilantro and mix all the ingredients well together. Cover and cook for 5–7 minutes.

Uncover the pan and stir-fry the cauliflower in its sauce for a further 2 minutes before serving.

Illustrated on page 33.

Cauliflower, Carrots and Potatoes in a Spicy Yogurt Sauce
(Masala Walay Dahee May Subzee)

This is a thoroughly spicy dish, perfect for adding interest to these rather mild vegetables.

½ CAULIFLOWER, BROKEN INTO SMALL FLOWERETS

2 POTATOES, DICED

2 CARROTS, SLICED

2 TEASPOONS SALT

1¼ CUPS CORN OIL

2 CUPS PLAIN YOGURT

1 TEASPOON SUGAR

1 TABLESPOON CHOPPED FRESH MINT

2 GREEN CHILES, FINELY CHOPPED

1 TABLESPOON CHOPPED FRESH CILANTRO

1 TABLESPOON CORN OIL

¼ TEASPOON MUSTARD SEEDS

4 CURRY LEAVES

Rub the vegetables with half the salt and set aside.

Heat the oil in a karahi or deep skillet to 375°F, or until a cube of bread browns in 30 seconds, add the salted vegetables and sauté them in the hot oil until cooked, but making sure they retain their texture and remain crunchy. Place the vegetables in a serving dish.

Blend the yogurt with the remaining salt, sugar, mint, green chiles and fresh cilantro and pour over the vegetables.

Heat the tablespoon of oil in a skillet, add the mustard seeds and curry leaves and sauté for about 1 minute. Pour the seasoned oil over the yogurt and vegetables and serve.

VARIATIONS
Spicy Yogurt Sauce with Zucchini, Broccoli and Green Beans
A very colorful version of the main recipe – use yellow or green-and-white striped zucchini if available. Substitute 2-3 zucchini and ½ lb green beans cut into 1-inch slices for the potatoes and carrots, and 2 large heads of broccoli, broken into flowerets, for the cauliflower. Proceed as in the main recipe.

Marrow and Pumpkin with Spicy Yogurt Sauce
Another colorful variation, especially if you can find the best variety of pumpkin – small, with dense, quite dry, very brilliant orange flesh and dark green skin. Substitute about 8–10 ounces peeled, deseeded and diced marrow and 8–10 ounces peeled, deseeded and diced pumpkin instead of the potatoes, carrots and cauliflower. Proceed as in the main recipe.

Zucchini and Carrots in Olive Oil
(Sarson Kay Thail May Subzee)

Olive oil, that staple of Mediterranean cooking, is not widely used in India as a cooking medium. It is more common as a beauty aid – combed through hair to make it healthy and glossy, or as a massage oil for babies. Interestingly enough, mustard oil, typically used in Bengali cuisine, is also used as a massage oil for babies. Unlike mustard itself, the oil is rich and mild. However – Indian cooks love to adopt fine ingredients such as olive oil, and this recipe is a perfect example. It is important not to overcook the zucchini, otherwise they will lose their shape and their delicate flavor.

2 LARGE ZUCCHINI, SLICED
2 LARGE CARROTS, SLICED
2 TABLESPOONS OLIVE OIL
2 BUNCHES SCALLIONS, CHOPPED
4 GARLIC CLOVES, HALVED
6–8 MINT LEAVES
1 TABLESPOON CHOPPED FRESH CILANTRO
1 TABLESPOON LEMON JUICE
2 TABLESPOONS VINEGAR
1 TABLESPOON SUGAR
1 TABLESPOON SALT
1 GREEN CHILE, FINELY CHOPPED

Blanch the zucchini and carrots in boiling water for about 3–5 minutes. Drain and set aside.

Heat the olive oil in a karahi or deep skillet and sauté the scallions and garlic cloves together for about 2 minutes. Stir in the zucchini and carrots, then the mint, cilantro, lemon juice, vinegar, sugar, salt and green chile.

Gently stir-fry until the vegetables are cooked, making sure the vegetables retain their shape.

Transfer to a serving dish and serve immediately.

Spicy Sautéed Peas and Corn
(Masala Matar Aur Bhutta)

This makes a very good side dish and is also very popular with children. Serve it together with a pulao or biryani, with a dhaal, some pickles and bread or poppadums.

10 BABY POTATOES, THICKLY SLICED
3 TABLESPOONS CORN OIL
1 ONION, DICED
2 CUPS FROZEN CORN
1½ CUPS FROZEN PEAS
1 TEASPOON SALT
1 TEASPOON CHILE POWDER
1 TABLESPOON CHOPPED FRESH CILANTRO
1 TABLESPOON LEMON JUICE
1 SWEET RED PEPPER, DESEEDED AND DICED
2 TOMATOES, SLICED

Blanch the baby potatoes for about 5 minutes in lightly salted boiling water, drain and set aside.

Heat the oil in a karahi or deep skillet, add the diced onion and stir-fry until golden brown.

Lower the heat and add the corn, peas, salt and chile powder and cook for 5–7 minutes, stirring occasionally to prevent it from catching at the bottom. Mix in the freshly chopped cilantro and the lemon juice, then add the potatoes and red pepper and cook for a further 5–7 minutes. Serve, garnished with the sliced tomatoes.

VARIATION
Spicy Sautéed Peppers and Carrots
Another delicious and colorful recipe to serve with this sauce. Substitute 10 ounces sweet red or yellow peppers, deseeded and finely diced, in place of the corn, and 8 ounces diced carrot instead of the peas. Proceed as in the main recipe.

RIGHT: *Spicy Sautéed Peas and Corn (recipe above, right) and Zucchini and Carrots in Olive Oil (recipe above). Zucchini are a variety of marrow or squash, so you could substitute either of those vegetables if preferred – or the attractive, pale green, pear-shaped chayotes, also known as "chow-chows" or "chokos."*

Vegetables in a Creamy Saffron Sauce
(Zafrani Subzee)

An ideal dish for a special dinner party. The vegetables are cooked in a rich aromatic sauce and should be served with Pea Pulao (see recipe on page 97). Saffron is a very elegant ingredient, in both taste and appearance, and its presence in a dish usually indicates a Mogul or Persian ancestry.

2 CUPS LIGHT CREAM

1 TABLESPOON TOMATO PASTE

1½ TEASPOONS GARAM MASALA

1 TEASPOON GINGER PULP

1 TEASPOON GARLIC PULP

1 TEASPOON CHILE POWDER

3 TABLESPOONS GROUND ALMONDS

¼ TEASPOON GROUND CINNAMON

¼ TEASPOON GROUND CARDAMOM

1 TEASPOON SALT

1¼ CUPS WATER

½ TEASPOON SAFFRON STRANDS, CRUSHED

⅓ CUP (¾ STICK) BUTTER

1 TABLESPOON OIL

1 ONION, DICED

¼ TEASPOON BLACK CUMIN SEEDS

3 ZUCCHINI, SLICED

3 CARROTS, SLICED

½ CAULIFLOWER, CUT INTO SMALL FLOWERETS

¾ CUP PEAS

1 TABLESPOON CHOPPED FRESH CILANTRO, TO GARNISH

Mix the cream, tomato paste, garam masala, ginger, garlic, chile powder, almonds, cinnamon, cardamom, salt, water and saffron strands together in a bowl and set aside.

Melt the butter with the oil in a medium-size saucepan over a medium heat. Add the diced onion and black cumin seeds and sauté for 3–5 minutes.

Add all the vegetables and stir-fry for a further 3 minutes before pouring in the sauce and stirring well to mix.

Lower the heat, cover and cook for 7–10 minutes.

Garnish the vegetables with fresh cilantro before serving.

Potato and Carrot Stir-fry
(Thalay Huway Aloo Aur Gajar)

A quick and easy last-minute recipe, perfect for family meals, or as an extra dish when you suddenly find you have an unexpected guest.

5 TABLESPOONS CORN OIL

4 CURRY LEAVES

1 TEASPOON FENNEL SEEDS

½ TEASPOON WHITE CUMIN SEEDS

1 TEASPOON CRUSHED DRIED RED CHILES

2 ONIONS, SLICED

1 TEASPOON GINGER PULP

1 TEASPOON GARLIC PULP

¼ TEASPOON TURMERIC

12 BABY POTATOES, CUT INTO ¼-INCH THICK SLICES

2 CARROTS

1 SWEET GREEN PEPPER, DESEEDED AND DICED

2 TABLESPOONS LEMON JUICE

2 RED CHILES, SLICED

Heat the oil in a heavy-bottom saucepan, add the curry leaves, fennel seeds, cumin seeds and dried red chiles and sauté for about 30 seconds.

Add the sliced onions and continue to stir-fry until some of the onion slices are darker than others. Lower the heat and gradually add the ginger, garlic and turmeric.

Add the vegetables, stirring continuously. Lower the heat to very low, cover the pan and steam-cook for 7–10 minutes.

When the vegetables are cooked, sprinkle on the lemon juice and serve, garnished with the sliced red chiles.

Hot and Spicy Cauliflower
(Mirch Masala Gobi)

A very spicy recipe from northern India.

2 ONIONS, SLICED

1 TEASPOON GARAM MASALA

1 TEASPOON GROUND CUMIN

1½ TEASPOONS GROUND CORIANDER

2 GREEN CHILES

1 TEASPOON GINGER PULP

1 TEASPOON SALT

¼ TEASPOON TURMERIC

1 TABLESPOON TOMATO PASTE

4 TABLESPOONS LEMON JUICE

4 TABLESPOONS OIL

½ TEASPOON WHITE CUMIN SEEDS

½ TEASPOON CORIANDER SEEDS, CRUSHED

4 DRIED RED CHILES

4 CURRY LEAVES

1 CAULIFLOWER, CUT INTO SMALL FLOWERETS

Place the sliced onions, garam masala, ground cumin, ground coriander, green chiles, ginger, salt, turmeric, tomato paste and lemon juice in a food processor, grind for about 1 minute and then set aside.

Heat the oil in a heavy-bottom saucepan, add the cumin seeds, coriander seeds, dried red chiles and curry leaves and sauté for about 30 seconds. Then add the onion and spice mixture to the pan and stir-fry for about 5 minutes.

Finally, add the cauliflower flowerets, cover the pan and cook over a low heat for 7–10 minutes, checking occasionally to prevent the mixture sticking to the bottom of the pan.

Serve the cauliflower hot with a dhaal (from the Beans, Peas and Lentils chapter on pages 76-89) and rice.

Spicy Stir-fried Cauliflower
(Thali Huwi Masala Gobi)

Cauliflower is a very good stir-fried vegetable. It cooks quickly, holds its shape, and its mild flavor is well enhanced by spices and aromatics. A favorite with Indian cooks.

¼ CUP CHANA DHAAL

½ TEASPOON MIXED FENNEL SEEDS,
CORIANDER SEEDS, WHITE CUMIN SEEDS

4 WHOLE DRIED RED CHILES

4 GARLIC CLOVES, SLICED

1 X 1½-INCH PIECE FRESH GINGER, SHREDDED

5 TABLESPOONS CORN OIL

1 BUNCH SCALLIONS, CHOPPED

½ SWEET GREEN PEPPER, DESEEDED AND SLICED

½ CAULIFLOWER, CUT INTO FLOWERETS

1 TEASPOON SALT

1 TEASPOON CHILE POWDER

2 TOMATOES, CUT INTO QUARTERS

2 TABLESPOONS CHOPPED FRESH CILANTRO

Pick over the chana dhaal (small yellow split peas) for any stones or other foreign bodies, then wash and drain them. Boil until soft but not mushy, drain, then set aside.

Mix the seeds, chiles, garlic and ginger together in a small bowl and set aside.

Heat the oil in karahi or deep skillet, lower the heat, add the whole spice mixture and sauté for about 1 minute. Add the scallions and sauté for 2–3 minutes, then add the green pepper, cauliflower, salt and chile powder, and continue to stir-fry gently for a further 5–7 minutes.

Finally, add the chana dhaal, tomato quarters and fresh cilantro. Blend the mixture together and transfer to a serving dish. Serve with Masala Puri (recipe on page 102).

VARIATION
Spicy Stir-fried Green Vegetables
Other vegetables may be substituted for the cauliflower, such as broccoli, broken into flowerets, peas, French beans, cut into 1-inch slices, and topped and tailed snow peas. Snow peas are not a typical Indian vegetable, but they lend themselves very well to this spicy stir-fry.

Other beans, such as black-eye beans, may be substituted for the yellow chana dhaal.

Vegetables in a Pasanda-style Sauce
(Subzee Kay Pasanday)

Pasanda sauces, typified by the use of yogurt, ground almonds and spices, are traditionally used in non-vegetarian dishes. However, when used with vegetables they are, if anything, even more delicious. They have their origins in Northern India, but are now so popular they are eaten all over the country, including in the vegetarian south. Some people like to dry-roast the spices before cooking, but these days spices are of such high quality that they are often used just as they are.

1 CUP PLAIN YOGURT

3 TABLESPOONS GROUND ALMONDS

2 TEASPOONS POPPY SEEDS

1 TEASPOON GARLIC PULP

1 TEASPOON GINGER PULP

¼ TEASPOON TURMERIC

1½ TEASPOONS CHILE POWDER

1 TEASPOON GARAM MASALA

4 GREEN CARDAMOM PODS

½ TEASPOON BLACK CUMIN SEEDS

4 TABLESPOONS CORN OIL

2 ONIONS, DICED

8 OUNCES CAN TOMATOES WITH THEIR JUICE

1 LARGE POTATO, DICED

1 CARROT, SLICED

1 BABY CAULIFLOWER, CUT INTO SMALL FLOWERETS

3 RED CHILES, SLIT DIAGONALLY

2 TABLESPOONS CHOPPED FRESH CILANTRO

⅔ CUP WATER

Beat the yogurt with a fork or a whisk and set aside.

In a saucepan dry-roast the ground almonds and poppy seeds, shaking the pan continuously, for about 1 minute. Remove from the heat and pour on to the yogurt. Then add the garlic, ginger, turmeric, chile powder, garam masala, the cardamoms and black cumin seeds.

Heat the oil in a heavy-bottom saucepan, add the onions and sauté until golden brown. Stir in the yogurt and spice mixture, lower the heat and sauté for 1–2 minutes. Pour in the tomatoes, stirring continuously. Add the vegetables, then the red chiles and fresh cilantro.

Stir in the measured water, lower the heat further, cover the pan and cook for 5–7 minutes, or until the vegetables are cooked through.

Serve the vegetables hot with a rice dish.

Green Chiles in Sesame Seeds
(Hari Mirch Aut Thill)

Try to choose the small but thick green chiles for this recipe as they are easier to seed. When slitting them, leave them intact at the top. Sesame's botanical name is "Sesamum indicum," which betrays its Indian origin. It is now widely used all over the world, but nowhere more widely than in India and China.

¾ CUP SESAME SEEDS

4 TABLESPOONS CORN OIL

15 GREEN CHILES, SLIT LENGTHWISE AND DESEEDED

¼ TEASPOON WHITE CUMIN SEEDS

3 DRIED RED CHILES

4 CURRY LEAVES

1½ TEASPOONS GROUND CORIANDER

1 TEASPOON GINGER PULP

1 TEASPOON GARLIC PULP

1 TEASPOON CHILE POWDER

2 TABLESPOONS LEMON JUICE

1 TABLESPOON CHOPPED FRESH CILANTRO

⅔ CUP WATER

Dry-roast the sesame seeds (see page 8) and grind them in a food processor or a spice grinder until they are powdery.

Heat the oil in a karahi or deep skillet, add the green chiles and sauté them for about a minute. Using a slotted spoon, remove from the oil and set aside.

Lower the heat and sprinkle the cumin seeds, dried red chiles and curry leaves into the pan. Sauté for 10 seconds. Remove the pan from the heat and add the ground sesame seeds, then the ground coriander, ginger, garlic, chile powder, lemon juice and fresh cilantro.

Return the pan to a very low heat and stir-fry, adding the water, for about 5 minutes. Finally, add the cooked green chiles and serve hot.

LEFT: From top, Green Chiles in Sesame Seeds (recipe above) and Vegetables in a Pasanda-style Sauce (recipe above, left).

Stuffed Tomatoes
(Aloo Bharay Tamatar)

Long-grain rice is used in this recipe rather than Basmati. Try to use a good quality long-grain rice as it is a delicious recipe.

⅓ CUP (¾ STICK) BUTTER

1 TABLESPOON OIL

1 ONION, DICED

½ TEASPOON BLACK CUMIN SEEDS

1 TEASPOON GINGER PULP

1 TEASPOON GARLIC PULP

1 TEASPOON CHILE POWDER

1 TABLESPOON TOMATO PASTE

1 TABLESPOON GROUND CORIANDER

1 CUP LONG-GRAIN RICE

⅓ CUP CORN

⅓ CUP SWEET GREEN PEPPER, DESEEDED AND DICED

⅓ CUP FROZEN PEAS

1 CARROT

1 TEASPOON SALT

3 TABLESPOONS LEMON JUICE

1 TABLESPOON CHOPPED FRESH CILANTRO

2 CUPS WATER

6–8 LARGE AND FIRM TOMATOES

TO GARNISH

2 POTATOES, THINLY SLICED

1 TEASPOON SALT

1 TEASPOON CRUSHED RED CHILES

OIL FOR DEEP-FRYING

2 FRESH CHILES

2 TOMATOES, SLICED

Heat the butter and oil in heavy-bottom saucepan, add the onion and cumin seeds and sauté until golden brown. Lower the heat, and stir in the remaining ingredients except the whole tomatoes and the garnish. Bring to a boil, lower the heat, cover the saucepan tightly and cook for 10–15 minutes.

Meanwhile, cut the tops off the tomatoes, scrape out the flesh and seeds and set the shells and tops aside.

When cooked, cool the rice mixture slightly and spoon it into the tomatoes. Put the tops on the tomatoes, place in an ovenproof dish and cook in a preheated moderate oven, 350°F, for 10–15 minutes.

Prepare the garnish; rub the potato slices with the salt and crushed red chiles. Heat the oil in a karahi or deep skillet to 350°F, or until a cube of bread browns in 30 seconds. Add the potato slices in batches and deep-fry until they are golden. Remove with a slotted spoon and drain on paper towels. Place the potato slices around the cooked tomatoes and garnish with the chiles and tomato slices.

Panir-stuffed Tomatoes
(Panir-Bharay Tamatar)

These tomatoes are filled with a spicy bean mixture, which, with the panir, makes them very nutritious. You could also serve them as an appetizer. You can buy panir from specialty shops, or make your own from the recipe on the opposite page.

¼ CUP BLACK-EYE BEANS

8–10 FIRM TOMATOES

4 TABLESPOONS CORN OIL

1 ONION, FINELY DICED

1 TEASPOON GROUND CORIANDER

1 TEASPOON GINGER PULP

1 TEASPOON CHILE POWDER

1 TEASPOON SALT

1 TEASPOON CHOPPED FRESH CILANTRO

⅓ CUP PANIR, CHOPPED INTO SMALL DICE

(SEE RECIPE, RIGHT)

1 TEASPOON LEMON JUICE

Boil the black-eye beans in lightly salted water until soft but not mushy. Drain and set aside.

Meanwhile, carefully cut the tops off the tomatoes and set aside. Remove the flesh from the tomatoes and put the tomato shells in an ovenproof dish.

Heat the corn oil and sauté the onions until golden brown. Lower the heat and add all the spices, including the salt, and the black-eye beans and blend together.

Add the fresh cilantro, panir and lemon juice. Stir-fry for 2–3 minutes and let cool.

Spoon the cooled mixture into the tomatoes. Cover with the tomato tops and bake in a preheated moderate oven, 350°F, for 15–20 minutes. Serve the tomatoes with chapatis or rice.

VARIATION
Panir-stuffed Zucchini or Acorn Squash
This recipe may be adapted to other vegetables, such as zucchini or acorn squash. Both these vegetables may need to cook a little longer in the oven than tomatoes. Test after 15 minutes, and cook longer, if required. Acorn squash is a variety of pumpkin, which is delicious with nutmeg, so you could also add ½ teaspoon ground nutmeg.

Stir-Fried Baby Onions with Panir

This makes an attractive dish for a dinner party. As it is a fairly dry dish, I suggest you choose any curry or dhaal which has a sauce to serve with it. You can buy panir from Asian specialty shops, or make your own, using the recipe on this page.

1 TABLESPOON CORN OIL

⅓ CUP (¾ STICK) BUTTER

1½ TEASPOONS GARAM MASALA

1 TEASPOON GARLIC PULP

1 TEASPOON GINGER PULP

1 TEASPOON SALT

1 TEASPOON CHILE POWDER

1 TABLESPOON TOMATO PASTE

15 BABY ONIONS, LEFT WHOLE

1 CUP PANIR, CUT INTO 1-INCH CUBES

(SEE RECIPE, RIGHT)

1 CUP CORN

¾ CUP PEAS

6 GREEN CHILES

2 TABLESPOONS CHOPPED FRESH CILANTRO

10–12 CHERRY TOMATOES

1 LIME, SLICED

Heat the corn oil and butter in a heavy-bottom saucepan. Turn the heat off so that the oil is cooled a little. While the oil is cooling, mix all the spices with the tomato paste and pour the mixture into the oil and butter. Turn the heat up to medium, add the whole onions and panir cubes and sauté for 3 minutes, stirring continuously.

Gradually add the corn and peas. Continuing to stir-fry, add the whole green chiles, freshly chopped cilantro and whole cherry tomatoes. Cover the pan and cook for about 3 minutes before serving, garnished with the lime slices.

Illustrated on page 32.

Panir ✓

Panir, also known as "paneer" is not a dish in itself – rather, it is an ingredient in many Indian dishes, vegetarian or otherwise. You will find it extensively used in recipes throughout this book. This is an ingredient which is very, very important in Indian cooking, especially vegetarian. Together with beans, peas and lentils, it is a major source of protein. It has been called "Indian cottage cheese," but I don't think this does it justice at all. Cottage cheese or ricotta could be used in some recipes (at a pinch), but the real thing is available in Asian supermarkets, and is not too much trouble to make yourself. Just allow enough time when you first try this recipe, and it will soon become second nature.

4½ CUPS WHOLE MILK, OR

HALF CREAM AND HALF WHOLE MILK

3 TABLESPOONS LEMON JUICE

Pour the milk into a saucepan, and bring to a boil. Remove from the heat and stir in the lemon juice. Bring back to a boil and keep stirring until the milk curdles.

Line a strainer with cheesecloth, and pour in the curdled milk. Bring the edges of the cheesecloth together and gently squeeze out the whey, or liquid part of the curdled milk. What is left is a rather crumbly kind of cheese, called "chena panir." You can use it in some salads and other dishes in this form, but I prefer it in its next stage, true panir. To achieve this, wrap the chena in cheesecloth, and shape into a rectangular block. Place a wooden board on top, and a weight (such as a tin of beans) on top of the board. After about 2 hours, the cheese will have firmed up and become panir.

Cut the panir into cubes and use as described in the recipes, which include:

Panir and Vegetable Samosas on page 30,

Vegetable Jalfrezi on page 36,

Vegetables in a Rich Creamy Sauce on page 38,

Shahi Panir Koftas on page 39,

Methi and Spinach Panir on page 47,

Panir with Mushrooms in a Creamy Sauce on page 50,

Fried Okra with Panir on page 51,

Stuffed Chiles on page 58,

Panir-stuffed Tomatoes on page 66 and

Stir-fried Baby Onions with Panir on page 67.

NOTE

An alternative, and perhaps easier way of making panir is to keep the chena wrapped in cheesecloth, put it back in the strainer, place a plate and weight on top and leave for 2 hours. The shape would not be as tidy as the rectangular block, but it is as easy to use as mozzarella.

Stuffed Green Chiles on Sautéed Onions
(Pyaaz Bhari Hari Mirch)

Try to choose the large thick variety of green chiles for this recipe. Not only are they easier to stuff, but they are sometimes not as hot as the thinner variety.

4 TABLESPOONS SESAME SEEDS

2 TEASPOONS GROUND CORIANDER

3 TEASPOONS MANGO POWDER

1 TEASPOON SALT

1 TEASPOON CHILE POWDER

3 TABLESPOONS LEMON JUICE

1 TEASPOON SOFT SUGAR

1 TABLESPOON WATER

10–12 GREEN CHILES

5 TABLESPOONS CORN OIL

½ TEASPOON ONION SEEDS

3 ONIONS, DICED

TO GARNISH

FRESH CILANTRO

LEMON WEDGES

Dry-roast the sesame seeds, shaking the saucepan all the time to prevent them from burning. Roast the seeds until some bits are darker than others. Remove the pan from the heat and transfer to a dish to cool.

Meanwhile, mix the ground coriander, mango powder, salt, chile powder, lemon juice, sugar and water together in a bowl.

Once the sesame seeds have cooled, put in a food processor or a spice grinder and grind until they are powdery. Blend them with the spice mixture; if you find that it is too dry, stir in a little water to make a very thick paste.

Prepare the green chiles by slitting them in the middle, making sure they remain intact at the ends.

Fill the split chiles with the spice mixture.

Heat the oil in a karahi or deep skillet, carefully add the stuffed chiles, about 4 at a time, and sauté until they are cooked. Remove from the oil and set aside.

Sauté the onion seeds and onions in the oil remaining in the pan over a medium heat for 5–7 minutes, then transfer to a serving dish. Place the cooked chiles on top of the onions and serve garnished with lemon wedges and fresh cilantro.

Bitter Gourds with Onions
(Karela Aur Pyaaz)

Bitter gourds, called karela in India, are probably the least-known Asian vegetable in the west. You will recognize them by their prickly green skins. It is important to soak them in salted water to draw out some of the very bitter taste.

2 BITTER GOURDS

2 TEASPOONS SALT

4 TABLESPOONS OIL

½ TEASPOON MUSTARD SEEDS

3 ONIONS, SLICED

1 TEASPOON GARLIC PULP

1½ TEASPOONS GROUND CORIANDER

1 TEASPOON GINGER PULP

¼ TEASPOON TURMERIC

1 TEASPOON CHILE POWDER

1 TEASPOON POPPY SEEDS

3 TABLESPOONS LEMON JUICE

2 FRESH RED CHILES, SLICED

1 TABLESPOON CHOPPED FRESH CILANTRO

Wash, peel and slice the bitter gourds. Rub the salt into the slices and set aside for about 2 hours.

Wash the bitter gourds under cold running water, rubbing them with your fingers to remove some of the seeds. Wash at least twice and set aside.

Heat the oil in a heavy-bottom saucepan, add the mustard seeds and sliced onions and sauté over a medium heat for about 4 minutes. Lower the heat and add the garlic, the ground coriander, ginger, turmeric, chile powder and poppy seeds. Stir well. Add the bitter gourd slices, then the lemon juice, red chiles and freshly chopped cilantro.

Continue to cook, stirring, for a further 3 minutes.

Cover the saucepan with a lid and cook for another 2 minutes before serving the bitter gourds with chapatis.

VARIATION

Cucumbers with Onions

If you are unable to buy bitter gourds in your grocery stores (though they are widely available now, even in supermarkets), this recipe is also delicious made with cucumbers. They should also be salted for 10–15 minutes before cooking, not because they are bitter, but because the salt will draw out some of the moisture in the vegetable so it will be firmer when cooked. Substitute 2 small or 1 large cucumber for the 2 bitter gourds, and proceed as in the main recipe.

RIGHT: *Illustrated here, from the top, are Stuffed Green Chiles on Sautéed Onions (recipe above) and Bitter Gourds (also known as Karela) with Onions (recipe above, right).*

Panir and Vegetable Roghan Josh

(Panir Aur Subzee Ka Roghan Josh)

You will love this tomato-based curry with its elegant, creamy sauce. Traditionally made with lamb, this dish has successfully been made vegetarian by using panir instead.

4 TABLESPOONS CORN OIL

1 CUP PANIR, CUBED (SEE PAGE 67)

⅔ CUP PLAIN YOGURT

½ CUP GROUND ALMONDS

1½ TEASPOONS GARAM MASALA

1 TEASPOON GARLIC PULP

1 TEASPOON GINGER PULP

1 TEASPOON CHILE POWDER

1½ TEASPOONS SALT

PINCH OF TURMERIC

6 TABLESPOONS OIL

1 X 1-INCH PIECE CINNAMON STICK

4 WHOLE BLACK PEPPERCORNS

4 WHOLE GREEN CARDAMOMS

1 BAY LEAF

1 LARGE ONION, SLICED

14 OUNCE CAN TOMATOES

2 TABLESPOONS LEMON JUICE

1 LARGE CARROT, SLICED

2 ZUCCHINI, SLICED

1 SWEET GREEN PEPPER, DESEEDED AND COARSELY DICED

⅔ CUP WATER

2 TABLESPOONS CHOPPED FRESH CILANTRO

2 GREEN CHILES, CHOPPED

FLAKED ALMONDS, TO GARNISH

Heat the oil in a karahi or deep skillet, add the panir cubes and sauté until it has some color, making it lightly crisp and golden on the outside. Remove with a slotted spoon and drain on paper towels.

Beat the yogurt, add the almonds, garam masala, garlic, ginger, chile powder, salt and turmeric. Set aside.

In a medium-size saucepan, heat the oil over a medium heat, add the whole spices and sauté for about 30 seconds, then add the onion and sauté until golden brown.

Pour the yogurt and spice mixture into the pan and stir-fry. Add the tomatoes and their juice and the lemon juice, followed by the carrot, zucchini and green pepper and continue to stir-fry over a medium heat for a further 2 minutes. Pour in the water, cover the pan and cook over a low heat for 3–5 minutes.

Uncover, stir in the cilantro, chiles and panir, spoon into a serving dish and garnish with flaked almonds.

Illustrated on page 123.

Potatoes and Leeks in a Creamy Sauce

Leeks are not very widely used in Indian cooking, but they are perhaps the mildest of the onion family. They originated in the Middle East, and are more closely identified with European cooking than Indian. However, this dish is not particularly spicy, so the rather delicate flavor of leeks can be more easily appreciated.

2½ CUPS WATER

10–12 BABY POTATOES, THICKLY SLICED

2 LEEKS, CLEANED AND SLICED

⅓ CUP (¾ STICK) BUTTER

1 TABLESPOON CORN OIL

½ TEASPOON FENNEL SEEDS

1 BAY LEAF

½ TEASPOON CORIANDER SEEDS, CRUSHED

½ TEASPOON BLACK PEPPERCORNS, CRUSHED

1 TEASPOON SALT

¾ CUP LIGHT CREAM

1 TABLESPOON CHOPPED FRESH CILANTRO

Bring the water to a boil, add the potatoes and leeks and blanch for about 5 minutes. Remove the pan from the heat, drain and set aside.

Heat the butter and oil in a heavy-bottom saucepan over a medium heat, add the fennel seeds, the bay leaf, crushed coriander seeds and black peppercorns and sauté for about 15 seconds.

Gradually add the potatoes and leeks and stir gently, being careful not to break the potato slices. Add the salt, cream and freshly chopped cilantro, cover the pan and cook for about 15 minutes more.

Check that the potatoes are cooked before transferring to a serving dish. This dish is good served as an accompaniment.

Potatoes with Peas
(Aloo Matar)

This is probably among the more popular vegetarian curries – there is hardly one which is better-known – and it is found on almost every Indian or Pakistani restaurant menu.

3 TABLESPOONS TOMATO PASTE

1 TEASPOON GROUND CORIANDER

1 TEASPOON CHILE POWDER

1 TEASPOON GARAM MASALA

1 TEASPOON GARLIC PULP

½ TEASPOON TURMERIC

1 TEASPOON SALT

1 TABLESPOON LEMON JUICE

3 TABLESPOONS CORN OIL

2 ONIONS, DICED

¾ CUP PEAS

1¼ CUPS CORN OIL

3 POTATOES, COARSELY DICED

2 TABLESPOONS CHOPPED FRESH CILANTRO

½ SWEET GREEN PEPPER, DESEEDED AND SLICED

½ SWEET RED PEPPER, DESEEDED AND SLICED

Mix the tomato paste, ground coriander, chile powder, garam masala, garlic, turmeric, salt and lemon juice together in a bowl and set aside.

Heat the corn oil in a skillet, add the onions and sauté until golden brown. Pour the tomato paste and spice mixture into the pan, lower the heat and stir-fry for about 3 minutes. Stir in the peas and set aside.

Heat the remaining corn oil in a karahi or deep skillet to 350°F, or until a cube of bread browns in 30 seconds, add the potatoes and sauté them until they have golden edges and are cooked through. Remove the potatoes dice from the pan and add to the peas and spice mixture.

Finally, add the fresh cilantro and sliced sweet green and red peppers and stir-fry for a further 2 minutes. Serve the dish hot.

Stir-fry Cabbage with Green Mango
(Thali Huwi Bund Gobi Aur Kairi)

The mangoes used in this stir-fry are green or unripe ones. They are used in cooked dishes in preference to the ripe ones because they have a sweet-and-sour taste. When mangoes first arrive at the grocery stores, they are very often green, sometimes needing many days to ripen. They can be used in the green, hard state, or you can buy special green mangoes in Asian and Caribbean grocery stores. There are hundreds of varieties of mango in India – and people have quite heated debates about which one is the best for this purpose or that. Be careful when peeling mangoes – they have a white, sticky sap, especially in the stalk, and it can burn your skin a little if you don't wash your hands immediately after peeling the fruit.

2 GREEN MANGOES

½ SMALL WHITE CABBAGE, GRATED FINELY

2 CARROTS, COARSELY GRATED

2 ONIONS, SLICED

1 LARGE SWEET RED PEPPER, DESEEDED AND SLICED

5 TABLESPOONS CORN OIL

1 TEASPOON MUSTARD SEEDS

4 WHOLE CURRY LEAVES

1 X 1½-INCH PIECE FRESH GINGER, SHREDDED

3 GREEN CHILES, SLICED LENGTHWISE

⅔ CUP WATER

1 TABLESPOON CHOPPED FRESH CILANTRO

Peel each mango, take out and discard the stone, and cut into two. Dice coarsely and put in a bowl with the cabbage, carrots, onions and red pepper.

Heat the oil in a heavy-bottom saucepan, add the mustard seeds, curry leaves and shredded ginger and sauté over a medium heat until they are a shade darker.

Stir in the green mangoes and vegetables and stir-fry for about 5 minutes. Add the green chiles and then, the water. Cover the pan and cook for 5–7 minutes.

Remove the lid, mix in the fresh cilantro, and serve hot, with chapatis, if you like.

Illustrated on page 123.

Aloo Saag

One of the best-known of all Indian vegetable dishes in the west. Aloo Saag – literally Potatoes and Spinach – is a winning combination in many different cuisines, but probably never better than in this dish.

5 TABLESPOONS CORN OIL

1 ONION, CHOPPED

4 CURRY LEAVES

6–8 FENUGREEK SEEDS

¼ TEASPOON ONION SEEDS

2 TOMATOES, SLICED

1 TEASPOON GARLIC PULP

1 TEASPOON CHILE POWDER

1½ TEASPOONS GROUND CORIANDER

1 TEASPOON SALT

1½ TEASPOONS MANGO POWDER

6–8 NEW POTATOES

½ LB FROZEN SPINACH

⅔ CUP WATER

2 RED CHILES, SLICED

3 TABLESPOONS CHOPPED FRESH CILANTRO

10–12 PIECES SHREDDED GINGER, TO GARNISH (OPTIONAL)

Heat the oil in a heavy-bottom saucepan and sauté the onion, curry leaves, fenugreek and onion seeds until they have changed color. Lower the heat to medium and add the tomatoes, garlic, chile powder, ground coriander, salt and mango powder.

Stir-fry for 3–5 minutes before adding the potatoes and spinach. Continue to stir-fry for a further 5 minutes.

Pour in the water, cover the pan and cook over a low heat for 10–15 minutes. When the potatoes are cooked through, add the red chiles and fresh cilantro. Mix thoroughly and transfer to a serving dish. Garnish with the shredded ginger pieces, if you like. This dish is best served with chapatis.

Stir-fried Mushrooms
(Thalay Huway Kumbi)

Though mushrooms are not very widely used in India, they are much appreciated by Indians living in other parts of the world. Use ordinary white, cultivated mushrooms, or varieties such as chestnut or brown cap. You could also substitute button mushrooms, which would give this dish a very attractive appearance – they will go a pretty yellow, thanks to the turmeric in the spices.

4 TABLESPOONS CORN OIL

2 ONIONS, SLICED

1 TEASPOON FENNEL SEEDS

¾ CUP PEAS

1 TEASPOON GARLIC PULP

¼ TEASPOON TURMERIC

2 GREEN CHILES

1 TEASPOON CHILE POWDER

1 TEASPOON SALT

2 TABLESPOONS CHOPPED FRESH CILANTRO

1 LB MUSHROOMS, THICKLY SLICED

Heat the oil in a deep skillet and sauté the onions and the fennel seeds for about 3 minutes, or until soft. Add the peas, garlic, turmeric, green chiles, chile powder and salt and stir-fry over a medium heat for another 3 minutes. Add the freshly chopped cilantro and mushrooms and continue to sauté for about 5 minutes, stirring gently, until the onions are cooked through.

Transfer the mushrooms to a serving dish and serve hot with puris or baby poppadums.

VARIATION
Stir-fried Snow Peas with Baby Corn
A delicious and colorful variation. Substitute 1 lb baby corn and ¼ lb snow peas for the mushrooms and peas. Add the baby corn at the same time as the fresh cilantro, and the snow peas about 1 minute before serving.

LEFT: *From the top, Aloo Saag (recipe above, left) and Stir-fried Mushrooms (recipe above). Mushrooms are not widely used in India, other than in Kashmir, in the far north-west. This dish is also delicious made with snow peas and baby corn.*

Vegetable Balti

Balti dishes have become very popular recently – the Indian dish of the moment. Their fame in Britain seems to have started in Birmingham, and from there balti houses seem to have sprung up in every large city. These dishes originate in Pakistan and in the area the British Raj knew as the North-west Frontier. They are named after the pan in which they are cooked – a double-handled, wok-like metal pot. You can also use an ordinary karahi, a wok or even a deep skillet. In restaurants, balti dishes are cooked and served in the same pan.

½ CUP BLACK-EYE BEANS

8 BABY POTATOES

1 LARGE CARROT, THICKLY SLICED

1 HEAD OF BROCCOLI, CUT INTO 8 SMALL FLOWERETS

7 TABLESPOONS CORN OIL

1 ONION, SLICED

½ TEASPOON ONION SEEDS

4 CURRY LEAVES

3 CLOVES GARLIC

2 TOMATOES, SLICED

1 TEASPOON CHILE POWDER

1 TEASPOON SALT

4 GREEN CHILES, THICKLY SLICED

1 TABLESPOON CHOPPED FRESH CILANTRO

Cook the black-eye beans in simmering water until soft.

Cook the potatoes and carrots in boiling salted water, then cut the potatoes in half. Set aside.

Heat the oil in a karahi or wok, add the onion, onion seeds and curry leaves, followed by the garlic.

Stir-fry for about 2 minutes, then add the tomatoes, chile powder and salt. Stir-fry for a further 30 seconds.

Add the potatoes, carrots and broccoli flowerets, then the black-eye beans. Continue to stir-fry for a further 3–5 minutes. Add the green chiles and fresh cilantro, cover with tinfoil and simmer for a further 2 minutes. Serve with accompaniments such as rice, naan or other Indian breads, dhaal and other vegetable dishes.

Balti Vegetables in a Spicy Sauce with Panir

An interesting variation on the basic vegetable balti. Panir, that special, easy-to-make-yourself Indian cheese, is wonderful for cooking. It holds its shape and doesn't melt into strings the way ordinary cheese does. It can be bought at Asian supermarkets, or made at home using the recipe on page 67. Feel free to experiment with balti dishes – many of the other stir-fried curries in this chapter can be happily adapted to the balti method of cooking.

4 TABLESPOONS CORN OIL

½ TEASPOON MUSTARD SEEDS

3 TABLESPOONS TOMATO PASTE

¾ CUP WATER

1 TEASPOON GRATED FRESH ROOT GINGER

½ TEASPOON CRUSHED FRESH GARLIC

1 TEASPOON GROUND CORIANDER

1 TEASPOON GARAM MASALA

1 TEASPOON SALT

½ TEASPOON BROWN SUGAR

1 CUP FROZEN PEAS

6-8 SMALL FLOWERETS OF CAULIFLOWER

1 ZUCCHINI, SLICED

1 CARROT, DICED

2 RED CHILES, SLICED

1 TABLESPOON CHOPPED FRESH CILANTRO

8–10 CUBES OF PANIR (SEE PAGE 67)

½ CUP LIGHT CREAM

Heat the corn oil in a karahi or wok, add the mustard seeds and cook for about 30 seconds. Lower the heat.

Beat the tomato paste with the water. Add the ginger, garlic, ground coriander, garam masala, salt and brown sugar. Pour into the karahai or wok, and stir continuously for about 2 minutes.

Add the vegetables, one by one, stirring to mix. Add the chiles, cilantro and panir and cook for a further 3 minutes. Pour in the cream, stir to blend, then serve.

Thali

Thalis are the most common vegetarian meals in India. Although native to South India, they are now found all over the sub-continent. You will find them in most restaurants, from the local version of a "three-star" to the simplest village "caff," where the usual metal tray may be supplanted by a banana leaf! You will even be served thalis when travelling by train, especially in the south – and very good they are too. Your order is taken at one station and telegraphed ahead to the next one. The thali is then freshly prepared and delivered to your seat at the next station. Briefly, a thali is usually served on a round metal tray with high sides, rather like a wide, shallow cake pan. In the center is a mound of rice, which is surrounded by "katoris" – small dishes of various curries, dhaals, chutneys, curd (yogurt) and other accompaniments. You flavor the rice with some or all of these dishes, according to taste or appetite. If you were ordering this dish in a restaurant, your plate would be constantly replenished until you had, literally, eaten all you could. Paan can be served at the end of any Indian meal, to freshen the palate after its adventures with so many different spices. They are often available in Asian specialty shops. If you are unable to find them, they may be omitted, or a small dish of dried fennel seeds substituted. Thalis are traditionally eaten with the fingers in India, but a spoon or fork does equally well if your "finger-food" skills are not very highly developed!

2 CUPS BASMATI RICE

3 CUPS WATER

½ TEASPOON SALT

KATORIS

A SELECTION OF KATORIS, FOR EXAMPLE:

RASAM (PAGE 82)

SAMBHAR (PAGE 84)

RAITA (PAGE 108)

CHUTNEYS OR PICKLES (PAGES 106–7)

CURRIES (PAGES 34–72)

CURD

2½ CUPS GREEK YOGURT, OR HOMEMADE YOGURT, MADE WITH

2½ CUPS WHOLE MILK AND

2 TABLESPOONS PLAIN YOGURT

OTHER ACCOMPANIMENTS

DHAAL

POPPADUMS

PURIS OR DOSAI (OPTIONAL)

FRESH RADISHES, FRESH CHILES,

LEMON WEDGES, SLICED TOMATOES

OR ONIONS (OPTIONAL)

PAAN, FENNEL SEEDS OR NUTS (OPTIONAL)

Rice

To prepare the rice, first wash it in several changes of water until the water runs clear. This removes the starches which would otherwise make the rice grains stick together. Cook in a rice-cooker, following the manufacturer's instructions.

Alternatively, wash the rice as described above, then place in a pan with water to the proportion of 2 cups of rice to 3 cups of water, and ½ teaspoon of salt. Bring to a boil, then cover and reduce the heat to the lowest temperature and simmer for about 25 minutes. Remove from the heat and rest, covered, for about 10 minutes more.

Katoris

Serve a selection of vegetable curries, pickles and chutneys, which could include those listed in the ingredients, or others from this book.

Curd

If using ready-prepared yogurt, spoon into small dishes and place on the thali. To prepare your own, bring the milk to a boil in a large pan, stirring constantly.

Remove from the heat and set aside to cool for 10 minutes. Skim any skin from the surface. Beat 2 tablespoons of yogurt in a small bowl, then stir into the warm milk. Beat further until the mixture is slightly frothy. Cover the bowl with a clean dish cloth and set aside in a warm place for 8 hours or overnight for the yogurt to thicken. Place in the refrigerator until it is ready to serve.

Dhaal

Choose any of the more liquid dishes in the Beans, Peas and Lentils chapter on pages 76-89.

Poppadums, Puris or Dosai

No thali would be complete without the popular crunchy breads, poppadums, available in a variety of spicy flavors from supermarkets. If you like, puris (see recipes on page 102) or dosai (see recipe on page 22) may also be included.

Fresh vegetables

Fresh salad vegetables such as radishes, tomato or lemon wedges, sliced onions or scallions, give a fresh, sharp contrast to the katoris. A few fresh chiles are often included.

Paan, Fennel Seeds or Nuts

Paan can be bought from Indian specialty shops in many flavor combinations. They are not an essential part of a thali and are something of an acquired taste.

To serve

Place a quantity of rice on the side of each tray. Working clockwise from the rice, place small dishes of katoris and dhaal around each thali tray, followed by poppadums, chutneys or pickles, and (if using), fresh vegetables, paan, fennel seeds or nuts. Diners add the other dishes to the rice, one by one according to taste. Serve extra rice separately.

Beans, Peas and Lentils

Lentils, split peas and dried beans are high in protein,
an essential element in well-balanced vegetarian
cooking. In this chapter you will find recipes for using
all these beans, peas and lentils in many different
dishes. Remember that beans, peas and lentils, are
best combined in a meal with a grain, such as rice
or bread, and perhaps a dairy product.

Masoor Dhaal with Vegetables
(Masoor Ki Dhaal Aur Subzee)

Masoor dhaal is the common split red lentil found in supermarkets all over the world.

½ CUP MASOOR DHAAL

½ CUP CORN OIL

¼ TEASPOON ONION SEEDS

6 WHOLE CURRY LEAVES

2 ONIONS, SLICED

1½ TEASPOONS GROUND CORIANDER

1 TEASPOON GINGER PULP

1 TEASPOON GARLIC PULP

1 TEASPOON CHILE POWDER

1½ TEASPOONS SALT

3 GREEN CHILES

1 POTATO, COARSELY DICED

3 TABLESPOONS CHOPPED FRESH CILANTRO

3 TOMATOES, SLICED

3–4 TABLESPOONS LEMON JUICE

Wash the masoor dhaal thoroughly before boiling it in unsalted water until soft but not mushy. Drain and set aside.

In a karahi or a deep skillet, with a lid heat the oil and sprinkle in the onion seeds and curry leaves. After 10 seconds, add the onions and sauté until golden brown.

Reduce the heat and add all the spices and salt.

Next, chop 2 of the green chiles, and add to the pan with the diced potato. Stir-fry for about 3 minutes before adding the dhaal, then the fresh cilantro, tomatoes and the remaining green chile, chopped. Blend the mixture together, then pour in the lemon juice, cover the pan and cook for 5–7 minutes.

Lentils with a Butter Dressing
(Tarica Dhaal)

Another recipe using masoor dhaal, this time with a butter dressing. Butter has a particular significance in India, where the cow is a sacred animal, and butter and clarified butter are used in religious ceremonies. Ghee, or clarified butter, is available in Asian specialty shops and some supermarkets. As described on page 46, you can also make your own by melting ordinary unsalted butter over a low heat. Simmer for about 45 minutes until the white milk solids separate out. Strain the clear golden ghee through cheesecloth before using.

¾ CUP MASOOR DHAAL

2½ CUPS WATER

1 TEASPOON GINGER PULP

½ TEASPOON GARLIC PULP

1 TEASPOON GROUND CORIANDER

1 TEASPOON SALT

½ TEASPOON TURMERIC

FOR THE BAGHAAR TARICA

1 TABLESPOON CORN OIL

⅓ CUP (¾ STICK) BUTTER

½ TEASPOON ONION SEEDS

3 WHOLE GARLIC CLOVES

1 ONION, SLICED

2 TOMATOES, SLICED

1 GREEN CHILE, CHOPPED

1 TABLESPOON CHOPPED FRESH CILANTRO, TO GARNISH

Wash the lentils. Place in a heavy-bottom saucepan, pour in the water, cover and bring to a boil. Add the ginger, garlic, ground coriander, salt and turmeric. Cover the saucepan again and cook slowly for 5 minutes. Remove the pan from the heat.

Using a wooden masher, mash the lentils. The dhaal should now have a consistency similar to thick soup. Spoon into a serving dish.

For the baghaar tarica, heat the oil and the butter in a skillet over a medium heat, add the onion seeds, garlic, onion, tomato and green chile and sauté for about 2 minutes. Remove the pan from the heat and pour over the dhaal.

Serve garnished with the freshly chopped cilantro.

PREVIOUS PAGES: *From left, Green Mango Dhaal (Kairi Ki Dhaal) (recipe page 79), and Bitter Gourds with Chana Dhaal (Karela Dhaal) (recipe page 84). Green or unripe Indian mangoes (known as "ambi" or "kairi") are available from around February to June or July and are used to give curries and various lentils a sweet/sour flavor. Bitter gourds should be salted before use, to draw out the bitter juices.*

Green Mango Dhaal
(Kairi Ki Dhaal)

There are hundreds of different varieties of mango in India. They are used ripe, to be eaten fresh or used in cooking, especially in chutneys. There is also a special variety of very juicy, sweet mango known rather bluntly as "sucking mangoes." You squeeze and knead the fruit until it is quite soft, then cut a small hole in one end and suck out the sweet juice – a good way of avoiding the fibrous strings you find in some varieties. Mangoes are also used green or unripe, when they are known as "ambi" or "kairi." These are available from about February to June or July and are used to give curries and various lentils a sweet/sour flavor. Mangoes often arrive in stores unripe, so you should be able to find them quite easily.

2 MEDIUM GREEN MANGOES

¾ CUP MASOOR DHAAL

5 TABLESPOONS CORN OIL

2 BUNCHES SCALLIONS, CHOPPED INTO 1½-INCH PIECES

4 GREEN CHILES, CHOPPED

½ TEASPOON WHITE CUMIN SEEDS

½ TEASPOON GINGER PULP

½ TEASPOON GARLIC PULP

1 TEASPOON CHILE POWDER

1 TEASPOON GROUND CORIANDER

2 TABLESPOONS CHOPPED FRESH CILANTRO

Wash, peel and coarsely slice the mangoes, discarding the pit. Put the mango slices in a bowl, cover and set aside.

Wash and inspect the lentils for any stones, etc. Boil the lentils in plenty of lightly salted water until soft but not mushy, drain and set aside.

Meanwhile, heat the oil in a heavy-bottom saucepan, add the scallions, mango slices, green chiles, cumin seeds, ginger and garlic and stir-fry, coating in the oil. Lower the heat and add the chile powder and ground coriander. Stir-fry for about 3–5 minutes. Add the cooked lentils and continue to stir-fry gently, being careful not to mash the dhaal, for about 1 minute.

Finally, add the fresh cilantro, cover the pan and cook for about 5 minutes over a very low heat.

Serve the Green Mango Dhaal hot.

Illustrated on page 76.

Whole Masoor Dhaal Khitchri

Khitchri, from Tamil Nadu in southern India, is the "grandfather" of that famous dish of the British Raj, kedgeree. This version is made with whole masoor, which is not as common as the split salmon-colored lentil, but it is delicious and has a very good texture.

2 CUPS BASMATI RICE

1 CUP WHOLE MASOOR DHAAL

3 TABLESPOONS CLARIFIED BUTTER

2 ONIONS, SLICED

¼ TEASPOON ONION SEEDS

¼ TEASPOON MUSTARD SEEDS

6 CURRY LEAVES

¼ TEASPOON TURMERIC

1 TEASPOON GINGER PULP

1 TEASPOON GARLIC PULP

1½ TEASPOONS SALT

6 DRIED RED CHILES

2 POTATOES, DICED

3 GREEN CHILES

4 CUPS WATER

Wash the rice and lentils together, drain them in a strainer and then set aside.

Melt the clarified butter in a medium-size saucepan, add the onions, onion seeds, mustard seeds and curry leaves and sauté for 2 minutes. Lower the heat and add the remaining spices.

Next, add the potatoes and green chiles and stir-fry for about 2 minutes before mixing in the rice and lentils. Using a slotted spoon, continue to stir-fry gently for another minute.

Pour in the water, bring to a boil, lower the heat, cover the pan, and cook for 15–20 minutes, or until the rice is tender and all the water has been absorbed.

Pasta with Snow Peas and Red Kidney Beans

Red kidney beans are sweet-tasting and the beans are often used in Mexican cooking. They are available dried or canned. Preparing them in their dried form can be a little complicated, so I find it much simpler and easier to use the canned variety.

2 OUNCES PASTA SHELLS

2 ONIONS, COARSELY DICED

2 TABLESPOONS TOMATO SAUCE

1 TEASPOON CHILE POWDER

1 TEASPOON GARLIC PULP

¼ TEASPOON TURMERIC

1½ TEASPOONS SALT

2 TABLESPOONS LEMON JUICE

1 TEASPOON SUGAR

½ CUP (1 STICK) BUTTER

1 TABLESPOON CORN OIL

½ TEASPOON ONION SEEDS

¼ LB SNOW PEAS, BLANCHED

2 TABLESPOONS CANNED RED KIDNEY BEANS, DRAINED

1 TABLESPOON FRESH CILANTRO

2 RED CHILES, SLICED

Cook the pasta in boiling salted water until it is tender. Drain and set aside.

Place the diced onions, tomato sauce, chile powder, garlic, turmeric, salt, lemon juice and sugar in a food processor or blender. Blend for about 1 minute or until a soft, smooth paste is formed.

Melt the butter with the oil and onion seeds in a deep skillet, add the spice mixture and sauté for about 5–7 minutes, stirring constantly. Add the pasta, then the snow peas, red kidney beans, fresh cilantro and red chiles and mix gently until well coated with the spice mixture.

Serve immediately with an Indian bread.

Baby Cauliflower with Toor Dhaal

This makes a very good dinner party dish, especially as good-quality baby vegetables are now readily available in supermarkets and grocery stores for much of the year.

3–4 BABY CAULIFLOWERS

2 TABLESPOONS TOOR DHAAL

1¼ CUPS WATER

4 TABLESPOONS OIL

4 CURRY LEAVES

¼ TEASPOON MUSTARD SEEDS

¼ TEASPOON FENUGREEK SEEDS

1 TEASPOON GARLIC PULP

1½ TEASPOONS CHILE POWDER

1 TEASPOON GINGER PULP

1½ TEASPOONS GROUND CORIANDER

¼ TEASPOON GROUND FENUGREEK

1 TEASPOON SALT

2 TABLESPOONS LEMON JUICE

3 RED CHILES, CHOPPED

2 TABLESPOONS CHOPPED FRESH CILANTRO

14 OUNCE CAN TOMATOES

TO GARNISH

3 TOMATOES, QUARTERED

2 LIMES, SLICED

Cook the baby cauliflowers whole in lightly salted boiling water until tender but still intact. Drain the cauliflowers and set aside on a serving dish.

Wash and pick over the lentils for any stones, etc, then cook them in the measured water until soft but not mushy. Drain and then set aside.

Heat the oil in a karahi or deep skillet, add the curry leaves, mustard seeds and fenugreek seeds and sauté briefly for about 30 seconds.

Mix the garlic, chile powder, ginger, ground coriander, ground fenugreek, salt, lemon juice, red chiles, fresh cilantro and the tomatoes with their juice in a bowl. Pour the mixture into the seasoned oil and stir-fry for 5–7 minutes over a low heat. Add the lentils and cook for a further 2 minutes.

Pour the mixture over the top of the cauliflower, garnish with the tomato quarters and lime slices and serve.

LEFT: *From top, Baby Cauliflower with Toor Dhaal (recipe above, right) and Pasta with Snow Peas and Red Kidney Beans (recipe above). Many supermarkets now stock baby vegetables such as cauliflowers, which make a very elegant dish. Though snow peas are not a traditional Indian vegetable, their fresh taste and texture are perfectly complemented by the spice mixture.*

Toor Dhaal with Tomatoes
(Tomatar Dhaal)

Toor dhaal, also known as "toovar dhaal," is a yellow split lentil, and there is also a pink variety. It has an interesting, dark, earthy flavor and is used in all the regions of India. You will sometimes find it coated in castor oil as a preservative, but this will be washed off when you boil it.

¾ CUP TOOR DHAAL

1 ¼ CUPS WATER

SALT

4 TABLESPOONS CORN OIL

1 TEASPOON MUSTARD SEEDS

14 OUNCE CAN TOMATOES

1 TEASPOON GINGER PULP

1 TEASPOON CHILE POWDER

1 TEASPOON GARLIC PULP

1 TEASPOON GROUND CUMIN

1 ½ TEASPOONS GROUND CORIANDER

¼ TEASPOON GROUND FENUGREEK

¼ TEASPOON GROUND FENNEL

1 ½ TEASPOONS SALT

2 TABLESPOONS LEMON JUICE

¼ CUP (½ STICK) BUTTER

1 SMALL ONION, CHOPPED

2 GREEN CHILES, CHOPPED

Wash the lentils and then boil in the lightly salted water until soft. When cooked, mash down to a paste, using a wooden masher. If necessary, add about 1 ¼ cups water to lighten the consistency.

Heat the oil in a heavy-bottom saucepan and gently sauté the mustard seeds.

Mix the canned tomatoes with their juice, the ginger, chile powder, garlic, ground cumin, ground coriander, fenugreek, fennel, salt and lemon juice in a small bowl and then add to the pan with the mustard seeds.

Stir-fry the mixture for 2 minutes, then add the mashed lentils and lower the heat to medium. Cook, partly covered, for about 1 minute.

Meanwhile, melt the butter in a skillet over a medium heat, add the chopped onion and green chiles and sauté for about 3 minutes.

Transfer the lentils to a warmed serving dish and pour the onion and chiles, with the butter in which they were cooked, over the lentils. Serve immediately.

Rasam

"Rasam" is the Tamil word for "essence," and this one is an essence of lentils, in this case toor dhaal. Eaten widely in South India, the basic rasam is flavored and seasoned with a variety of spices and other ingredients, which can include ginger, mustard seeds, chiles, peppercorns, cumin, asafetida, curry leaves and, often, the cooling edge of tamarind.

¼ LB RED TAMARIND BLOCK

⅔ CUP HOT WATER

¾ CUP TOOR DHAAL

3 CUPS WATER

1 TEASPOON SALT

¼ TEASPOON TURMERIC

1 TEASPOON GROUND CUMIN

1 ½ TEASPOONS GROUND CORIANDER

¼ TEASPOON BLACK PEPPERCORNS, CRUSHED

½ TEASPOON CRUSHED DRIED RED CHILES,

1 TEASPOON GARLIC PULP

2 TOMATOES, QUARTERED

2 TABLESPOONS CORN OIL

½ TEASPOON WHITE CUMIN SEEDS

6 CURRY LEAVES

3 FRESH GREEN CHILES

Break down the tamarind block. Pour the hot water over the tamarind and leave it to soak for about 10-15 minutes. Squeeze out all the water and push the tamarind through a strainer to extract the pulp.

Wash the lentils, put in a saucepan with the measured water, bring to a boil and cook over a medium heat. When the lentils are soft, add the salt, turmeric, ground cumin, ground coriander, crushed black peppercorns, chiles and garlic and then mash the dhaal down with a wooden masher.

Add the tomato quarters and the tamarind pulp and cook for about 2 minutes.

Meanwhile, heat the corn oil in a saucepan, add the cumin seeds, curry leaves and green chiles and sauté for 1 minute. Pour the mixture over the dhaal. Serve hot.

Toor Dhaal with Scallions

Scallions are best used fresh or very quickly stir-fried, as in Chinese or Vietnamese cooking. This is the way they are used in this colorful dish – a lively counterpoint to the tomatoes, sweet green pepper and green chiles.

½ CUP LENTILS (TOOR DHAAL)

2 CUPS WATER

4 TABLESPOONS OIL

¼ TEASPOON WHITE CUMIN SEEDS

4 GARLIC CLOVES, SLICED

2-INCH PIECE FRESH GINGER, SHREDDED

4 DRIED RED CHILES

1 LARGE BUNCH SCALLIONS, CHOPPED

2 TOMATOES, CHOPPED

1 SWEET GREEN PEPPER, DESEEDED AND SLICED

2 GREEN CHILES, FINELY CHOPPED

2 TABLESPOONS LEMON JUICE

1 TEASPOON SALT

1 TABLESPOON CHOPPED FRESH CILANTRO

Boil the lentils in the measured water until they are soft but not mushy and set aside.

Meanwhile, heat the oil in a saucepan, add the whole cumin seeds and sauté for 10 seconds, then lower the heat and add the garlic, ginger, dried red chiles, scallions, tomatoes, sweet green pepper and green chiles and stir-fry for about 3 minutes.

Pour the lentils over the mixture and continue to stir-fry for a further 2 minutes before adding the lemon juice, salt and the chopped fresh cilantro.

Serve the toor dhaal hot with chapatis.

VARIATIONS

This recipe can also be made in a number of different ways. Instead of the toor dhaal, you could substitute a similar quantity of chick peas, black-eye beans, red kidney beans, or a mixture of all three to produce a very colorful dish. You could also substitute ordinary diced onions or finely sliced leeks for the chopped scallions.

Lentil and Vegetable Patties

These patties can either be served as a snack any time of day or as part of a vegetarian meal. If you decide to serve them as a snack, serve with one of the chutneys from this book.

1 TABLESPOON TOOR DHAAL

2 POTATOES, DICED

2 CARROTS, DICED

1 ONION, DICED

½ CAULIFLOWER, CUT INTO SMALL FLOWERETS

2 GREEN CHILES, CHOPPED

1 TABLESPOON CHOPPED FRESH CILANTRO

2 TABLESPOONS CORN OIL

¼ TEASPOON ONION SEEDS

1 TEASPOON GINGER PULP

1 TEASPOON GARAM MASALA

1 TEASPOON CHILE POWDER

1½ TEASPOONS SALT

1 TABLESPOON LEMON JUICE

OIL FOR SHALLOW-FRYING

Wash the lentils and boil in lightly salted water until soft but not mushy. Remove from the heat and set aside (still in the cooking water) while preparing the rest of the ingredients.

Put the potatoes, carrots, onion, cauliflower, green chiles and fresh cilantro into a saucepan with water to cover and cook until the vegetables are soft. Drain and set aside.

Heat the oil in a karahi or a deep skillet, add the onion seeds and sauté until they turn a shade darker. Add the cooked vegetables, the drained lentils, ginger, garam masala, chile powder, salt and lemon juice. Stir so that all the ingredients are combined well together.

Transfer the mixture into a large bowl and let cool.

Using a fork, break off small balls from the mixture, about the size of a golf ball, and flatten in the palm of your hands to form small patties. You should get about 10–12 patties.

If the patty mixture seems to break apart easily, add about 1 tablespoon of all-purpose flour to the mixture to help the patties stay together.

Once you have made the lentil patties, heat the oil in a skillet, add the patties in batches and sauté over a medium heat, turning them at least once.

Serve the Lentil and Vegetable Patties hot.

Sambhar

A typical southern Indian lentil dish that is probably made every day in most southern Indian homes. It can also be made using masoor dhaal (split red lentils), urid dhaal, or a mixture of chick peas and urid dhaal. Vary the lentil variety according to taste.

¾ CUP TOOR DHAAL

1½ TEASPOONS GROUND CORIANDER

¼ TEASPOON TURMERIC

1½ TEASPOONS CHILE POWDER

¼ TEASPOON GROUND FENUGREEK

3¾ CUPS WATER

6 SMALL CAULIFLOWER FLOWERETS

¼ LB FROZEN GREEN BEANS

2 TOMATOES, QUARTERED

2 GREEN CHILES, CHOPPED

1½ TEASPOONS SALT

6 BABY ONIONS, PEELED

1 TABLESPOON TAMARIND PASTE

1 TABLESPOON BROWN SUGAR

FOR THE BAGHAAR TARICA

4 TABLESPOONS CORN OIL

¼ TEASPOON MUSTARD SEEDS

6 WHOLE CURRY LEAVES

LARGE PINCH OF WHITE CUMIN SEEDS

4 DRIED RED CHILES

3 GARLIC CLOVES

PINCH OF ASAFETIDA

FRESH CILANTRO, TO GARNISH

Wash the toor dhaal, place in a heavy-bottom saucepan and add the ground coriander, turmeric, chile powder, ground fenugreek and water. Cover the pan and cook the mixture over a medium heat, stirring occasionally to prevent it overflowing.

Once the toor dhaal is soft enough to be mashed, mash it down in the saucepan. If the dhaal is too thick, add another ½ cup of water to loosen the consistency.

Next, add the cauliflower, beans, tomatoes, green chiles, salt, baby onions, tamarind paste and brown sugar and bring to a boil. Lower the heat and simmer gently for a further 10 minutes. Adjust the consistency and seasoning to taste. Transfer to a serving dish and set aside.

Meanwhile, make the baghaar tarica. Heat the oil in a skillet, add the mustard seeds, curry leaves, cumin seeds, dried red chiles, garlic and asafetida and sauté until everything turns a shade darker. Pour the hot baghaar over the toor dhaal.

Serve garnished with the fresh cilantro.

Bitter Gourds with Chana Dhaal
(Karela Dhaal)

Karela, or bitter gourd, is a vegetable with a very distinctive bitter taste. You prepare it as you would cucumber for cooking. Cut in half lengthwise, scoop out the seeds and sprinkle the flesh with salt to draw out some of the bitter juices before cooking. Alternatively, just take off the rough part of the skin, leaving the seeds in, then chop the flesh into large dice before salting. Delicious and delicate with dhaal.

2 BITTER GOURDS, ABOUT 5-INCHES LONG

1 TABLESPOON SALT

½ CUP CHANA DHAAL

2 ONIONS, SLICED

1 TEASPOON GINGER PULP

1 TEASPOON CHILE POWDER

1 TEASPOON GARLIC PULP

1 TEASPOON GARAM MASALA

1 TEASPOON GROUND CORIANDER

1½ TEASPOONS SALT

2½ CUPS WATER

4 TABLESPOONS CORN OIL

2 TOMATOES, SLICED

TO GARNISH

1-INCH PIECE FRESH GINGER, SHREDDED

½ TEASPOON GARAM MASALA

1 TABLESPOON FRESH CILANTRO

1 GREEN CHILE, SLICED

Wash the bitter gourds and pat dry with paper towels. Peel off the rough skins and slice the gourds, discarding the seeds. Place the sliced gourds in a bowl, rubbing the salt into the slices. Set aside for about 1 hour.

Meanwhile, wash the chana dhaal and place in a saucepan. Add 1 of the sliced onions, the ginger, chile powder, garlic, garam masala, ground coriander, salt and water and cook over a medium heat, partly covered, for 15–20 minutes or until the dhaal is soft but not mushy, and all the water has been absorbed. Remove from the heat and set aside.

Wash the bitter gourds thoroughly to remove all the salt and add to the dhaal.

Heat the corn oil in a deep skillet and sauté the remaining sliced onion until golden brown. Add the sliced tomatoes and the dhaal and stir-fry for about 3 minutes to blend together.

Transfer to a serving dish and serve garnished with shredded ginger, garam masala, fresh cilantro and sliced green chile.

This dish goes well with hot chapatis or puris.

Illustrated on page 77.

Masala Urid Dhaal

Urid is a small lentil with a black skin, closely related to moong dhaal. There are two varieties of urid dhaal – the skinned kind, which are creamy-white in color, and the unskinned kind, with black husks, split, so they show their pale interiors. The type of urid lentil used in this recipe is the whole one with the husks removed. It is readily available in Asian specialty shops.

1 CUP URID DHAAL

2 TABLESPOONS CLARIFIED BUTTER

1 LARGE ONION, SLICED

1½-INCH PIECE FRESH GINGER, SHREDDED

4 GARLIC CLOVES, SLICED

2 GREEN CHILES, SLICED

2 RED CHILES, SLICED

½ TEASPOON ONION SEEDS

1 TABLESPOON LEMON JUICE

1 TABLESPOON CHOPPED FRESH CILANTRO

1 TABLESPOON FRESH MINT

MASALA

½ TEASPOON GROUND CUMIN

½ TEASPOON GROUND CORIANDER

½ TEASPOON BLACK SALT

¼ TEASPOON CITRIC ACID

Boil the lentils in 2½ cups of lightly salted water until soft but not mushy. Drain and place in a serving dish.

Melt the clarified butter in a skillet over a high heat, add the onion and sauté until golden brown. Lower the heat to medium and add the ginger, garlic, green and red chiles, onion seeds and lemon juice, stirring constantly.

Pour the mixture over the dhaal in the serving dish and garnish with the fresh cilantro and mint.

Mix the masala ingredients together in a small bowl and sprinkle over the dhaal.

Serve with freshly made chapatis.

Spicy Chick peas
(Chana Masala)

This recipe uses canned chick peas, which I find is a much more convenient way of using this delicious pea, rather than starting from the beginning with dried ones. If you prefer to use the dried ones however, soak them in the usual way – in cold water for at least 12 hours or overnight. It is a good idea to change the soaking water several times during this period if possible. When soaked, drain the chick peas and, for about 1 lb dry weight, cover with 9 cups of cold water. Bring to a boil, skim the froth off the top, then simmer for 2–3 hours, or until tender. Add salt about halfway through the cooking time.

2 ONIONS, CHOPPED

1½ TEASPOONS GARAM MASALA

1 TEASPOON CHILE POWDER

2 TEASPOONS GROUND POMEGRANATE SEEDS

½ TEASPOON GARLIC PULP

1 TEASPOON SALT

2 TABLESPOONS TOMATO PASTE

3 TABLESPOONS CORN OIL

2 GARLIC CLOVES

1 INCH PIECE FRESH GINGER, SHREDDED

½ TEASPOON WHITE CUMIN SEEDS

15 OUNCE CAN CHICK PEAS, DRAINED

TO GARNISH

1 TABLESPOON CHOPPED FRESH CILANTRO

2 TOMATOES, SLICED

2 GREEN CHILES, SLICED

1 SMALL ONION, SLICED IN RINGS

Place the onions in a food processor with the garam masala, chile powder, ground pomegranate seeds, garlic, salt and tomato paste and blend for about 20 seconds.

Heat the oil in a karahi or deep skillet, add the garlic cloves and shredded ginger and sauté for about 10 seconds before adding the cumin seeds. Sauté these for 10 seconds, lower the heat and add the onion mixture to the pan.

Stir-fry for about 3 minutes to cook the spices, then add the chick peas. Continue to cook for a further 5–7 minutes.

Transfer the dhaal to a serving dish and garnish with the fresh cilantro, sliced tomato, green chiles and onion rings.

Spicy Tomatoes and Eggplants with Chick peas

Chick peas are a favorite ingredient in Middle Eastern and Mediterranean cooking, as well as Indian. There, too, they are teamed with tomatoes and eggplants, which just goes to emphasize that some ingredients seem made for each other. Chick peas are a very good source of protein for vegetarians and they become a beautiful golden yellow when cooked, making this a colorful and attractive dish for entertaining.

5 TABLESPOONS CORN OIL

1 ONION, DICED

1 TEASPOON GINGER PULP

¼ TEASPOON TURMERIC

1 TEASPOON GARLIC PULP

1 TEASPOON GARAM MASALA

1½ TEASPOONS GROUND CORIANDER

1 TEASPOON CHILE POWDER

14 OUNCE CAN TOMATOES

1 SMALL EGGPLANT, DICED

1 SWEET ORANGE PEPPER, DESEEDED AND DICED

8 OUNCE CAN CHICK PEAS, DRAINED

1–1½ TEASPOONS SALT

Heat the corn oil in a karahi or deep skillet, add the diced onion and sauté until golden brown. Lower the heat and stir in the ginger, turmeric, garlic, garam masala, ground coriander and chile powder.

Pour in the tomatoes and their juice, then the eggplant, sweet orange pepper, chick peas and salt to taste. Stir-fry for about 5–7 minutes, trying not to break the chick peas.

Serve hot with a rice dish.

VARIATION

Substitute black-eye beans, dried butter beans or dried navy or flageolet beans for the chick peas. If you would prefer to use dried chick peas rather than canned, prepare the dried ones as described in the introduction to the recipe on page 85.

Spicy Black-eye Beans
(Masala Lobia)

Black-eye beans have a wonderful earthy flavor and excellent texture. Also known as black-eyed peas, they are a variety of cow peas, and are widely used in Caribbean and southern American cooking. They are easily identified by the distinctive black "eye" on top of the cream-colored kidney-shaped bean. Although black-eye beans are quite widely available, you could also make this dish with dried or canned navy beans or butter beans.

1 CUP BLACK-EYE BEANS

5 TABLESPOONS CORN OIL

2 ONIONS, SLICED

1 TEASPOON GINGER PULP

1 TEASPOON GROUND CORIANDER

1½ TEASPOONS CHILE POWDER

½ TEASPOON TURMERIC

2 TOMATOES, CHOPPED

½ TEASPOON SALT

2 TABLESPOONS LEMON JUICE

2 GREEN CHILES

TO GARNISH

1¼ CUPS OIL

8–10 BABY POTATOES, SLICED

1 TABLESPOON CHOPPED FRESH MINT

1 TEASPOON GARAM MASALA

Wash the black-eye beans and cook in boiling water until soft. Drain and set aside.

Heat the corn oil in a large skillet, add the sliced onions and sauté until golden brown. Lower the heat and add the ginger, ground coriander, chile powder, turmeric, chopped tomatoes and salt. Stir-fry for about 2 minutes.

Carefully tip in the black-eye beans and mix together. Add the lemon juice and green chiles, stir to mix and transfer to a serving dish.

For the garnish, heat the oil in a deep skillet to 375°F, or until a cube of bread browns in 30 seconds, add the potato slices and sauté until cooked. Arrange the potato slices on top of the black-eye beans and garnish the dish with the mint. Sprinkle the garam masala over the top before serving.

RIGHT: *From top, two easily prepared bean, pea and lentil dishes, Spicy Black-eye Beans – Masala Lobia – (recipe above, right) and Spicy Tomatoes and Eggplants with Chick peas (recipe above).*

Black-eye Beans

*Black-eye beans cook very quickly, and do not require
pre-soaking – an excellent ingredient to choose for a quick
meal. The slightly smoky, earthy flavor of these beans goes
very well with vegetables such as eggplants and tomatoes,
and so do chick peas, as shown in the variation below.*

1 CUP BLACK-EYE BEANS

4 TABLESPOONS CORN OIL

1 ONION, CHOPPED

1 TEASPOON CHILE POWDER

3 TABLESPOONS LEMON JUICE

1½ TEASPOONS GROUND CORIANDER

1½ TEASPOONS SALT

3 GREEN CHILES

3 TABLESPOONS CHOPPED FRESH CILANTRO

2 TOMATOES, SLICED

1 LEMON, SLICED

Wash the black-eye beans and boil in plenty of water until
soft. Drain and set aside in a bowl.

Heat the oil in a heavy-bottom saucepan, add the chopped
onion and sauté over a medium heat. Lower the heat, then add
the chile powder, lemon juice, ground coriander and salt. Pour
in the black-eye beans and stir-fry. Switch the heat off, then
cover and set aside.

Place the green chiles and the fresh cilantro in a food
processor and blend for 30 seconds.

Transfer the beans to a serving dish and mix in the green
chiles and cilantro mixture.

Garnish with the sliced tomatoes and lemon slices and serve.

VARIATION

Chick peas with Eggplants

Substitute a similar quantity of canned chick peas for the
black-eye beans and add an eggplant as well as the tomatoes.
Slice the eggplant, sprinkle with salt to drain out the bitter
juices. Set aside for 30 minutes then rinse and pat dry. Proceed
as in the main recipe.

Dried chick peas may also be used. Before using them in this
recipe, soak them in cold water overnight, changing the water
several times if possible, then cook in the following way.

Place the chick peas in a saucepan with cold water to cover.
Bring to a boil and skim the foam which rises to the surface.
Reduce the heat and simmer gently for 2–3 hours (the length of
time will depend on the age of the chick peas). Add salt about
halfway through the cooking time. Drain, then proceed as in
the main recipe.

Baby Potatoes with Navy Beans

*Navy beans are not widely used in Indian cooking, although
they marry perfectly with these spices and aromatics.
Like so many other interesting vegetables, they were
introduced to Europe from North America in the
16th century, and enthusiastically adopted by the French.
Navy beans are very nutritious and contain more protein
than meat, so are very valuable in a vegetarian diet.
Flageolet beans were developed from them in the middle of
the last century, and could also be used in this recipe; they
are available canned or dried.*

15 BABY POTATOES

½ CUP NAVY BEANS, CANNED OR FROZEN

1 CUP PLAIN YOGURT

1 TEASPOON GINGER PULP

1 TEASPOON GARLIC PULP

1 TABLESPOON TOMATO PASTE

1½ TEASPOONS GARAM MASALA

1 TEASPOON CHILE POWDER

1 TEASPOON SALT

½ TEASPOON GROUND FENNEL SEEDS

4 TABLESPOONS OIL

2 BAY LEAVES

1 LARGE ONION, DICED

2 TABLESPOONS CHOPPED FRESH CILANTRO

2 TOMATOES, QUARTERED

Boil the baby potatoes in lightly salted water until cooked,
drain and set aside. Drain or thaw the navy beans, depending
on which kind you are using.

In a bowl, mix the yogurt, ginger, garlic, tomato paste, garam
masala, chile powder, salt and ground fennel seeds. Mix
together thoroughly and set aside.

Heat the oil in a saucepan, add the bay leaves and onion and
sauté for about 5 minutes over a medium heat.

Stir the yogurt and spice mixture into the onions and stir-fry
for 3–5 minutes, or until the sauce has thickened. Add the
potatoes and beans and half the fresh cilantro. Continue to
stir-fry gently, trying not to break up the vegetables.

Once the sauce has thickened and has a semi-dry texture, stir
in the remaining fresh cilantro and quartered tomatoes.

Cook for a further 2 minutes over a low heat and serve hot
with puris.

VARIATION

This recipe can also be made with dried white navy or green
flageolet beans. Soak in water overnight, drain, then cover with
cold water, bring to a boil and simmer until tender. Proceed as
in the main recipe.

Fava Beans with Scallions

I would suggest you cook this dish in butter. Though fava beans are not widely used in India, they are delicious this way.

2 TABLESPOONS BUTTER

1 TABLESPOON OIL

½ TEASPOON ONION SEEDS

3 BUNCHES SCALLIONS, CHOPPED

3 RED CHILES, CHOPPED COARSELY

1 SWEET GREEN PEPPER, SLICED

½ TEASPOON GARLIC

½ TEASPOON GINGER

1 TEASPOON CHILE POWDER

1 TABLESPOON LEMON JUICE

15 OUNCE CAN FAVA BEANS, DRAINED

1 CUP SLICED MUSHROOMS

2 TABLESPOONS FRESH CILANTRO

1 TEASPOON SALT

Heat the butter with the oil and sauté the onion seeds for 30 seconds, then add the scallions and sauté until soft.

Add half the red chiles, the green pepper, garlic, ginger, chile powder and lemon juice to the pan. Stir-fry for 2 minutes, then lower the heat, add the fava beans and stir-fry.

Next add the mushrooms, cilantro and salt. Stir in the remaining red chiles, stir-fry for 3–5 minutes and serve hot.

Chohlay

This is a very popular snack or part of a vegetarian meal.

15 OUNCE CAN CHICK PEAS, DRAINED

1 LARGE POTATO, CUBED AND BOILED

2 TEASPOONS POMEGRANATE SEEDS

1 TEASPOON SUGAR

2 TABLESPOONS LEMON JUICE

1 TEASPOON GROUND CORIANDER

½ TEASPOON GARAM MASALA

1 TEASPOON CHILE POWDER

1 ONION, FINELY DICED

2 GREEN CHILES

1 TABLESPOON FRESH CILANTRO

2 TOMATOES

Put the chick peas and potato in a bowl. Roast the pomegranate seeds and grind in a spice grinder. Mix the seeds with the sugar, lemon juice, coriander, garam masala and chile powder, then pour over the chick peas; mix well. Add the onion, garnish with green chiles, cilantro and tomato. Serve hot or cold.

Baby Corn and Mushrooms with Moong Dhaal

Vegetables such as corn, native to the Americas, were unknown in India until introduced by the Portuguese, probably in the 16th century. Corn and other New World vegetables have been enthusiastically adopted there, as in Europe. Baby corn is widely available in supermarkets and Asian specialty shops and is fresh and delicious in this stir-fried lentil dish.

¼ CUP MOONG DHAAL

4 TABLESPOONS CORN OIL

2 ONIONS, DICED

1 TEASPOON GROUND CORIANDER

2 TEASPOONS MANGO POWDER

1 TEASPOON CHILE POWDER

¼ TEASPOON TURMERIC

1 TEASPOON SALT

1 CUP BABY CORN

⅔ CUP FROZEN PEAS

2 CUPS MUSHROOMS

Boil the moong dhaal in lightly salted water until soft but not mushy. Drain, place in a bowl and set aside.

Heat the oil in a heavy-bottom saucepan, add the diced onions and sauté until golden brown.

Meanwhile, mix together the ground coriander, mango powder, chile powder, turmeric and salt in a small bowl and pour the mixture into the cooked onions. Lower the heat immediately and stir-fry for about 1 minute.

Add the baby corn, peas and mushrooms and continue to stir-fry for a further 3–5 minutes.

Mix in the moong dhaal and serve immediately, accompanied by freshly made paratas (see recipe on page 103).

Rice

The ideal rice for Indian dishes is Basmati – a fine,
long-grained rice with a delicate perfume. Basmati rice
must be picked over, washed and well drained before
use. This process is not necessary with a packaged
American rice, though it will have a better
texture if it is washed.

Aromatic Rice

Rice is the basis of most Indian meals, vegetarian or otherwise, especially in the south. Basmati is the variety most highly regarded, but it can be very delicate and should be handled carefully during cooking. Because the rice is the focal point of this dish, I think it is worth using the very best quality you can find. If Basmati is not available, any other good, long-grained rice can be substituted, including Patna or American long-grain rice. When preparing rice, you must always wash it in several changes of cold water until it runs clear. This will rinse away the cloudy starch particles which would otherwise make the rice sticky. This rice is very simple to cook and is made using only whole spices.

2 CUPS BASMATI RICE

½ CUP (1 STICK) UNSALTED BUTTER

1 TABLESPOON CORN OIL

1 TEASPOON MUSTARD SEEDS

4 WHOLE DRIED RED CHILES

6 CURRY LEAVES

1½-INCH PIECE OF FRESH GINGER, SHREDDED

3 GARLIC CLOVES, SLICED

1 TEASPOON SALT

3 CUPS WATER

Wash the rice until the water runs clear, drain and set aside.

Melt the butter and oil in a heavy-bottom saucepan over a medium heat, add mustard seeds, dried red chiles, curry leaves, ginger, garlic and salt and sauté for about 2 minutes.

Add the rice and stir-fry gently for another minute, then pour in the water. Increase the heat and bring to a boil. Lower the heat to medium, cover the saucepan and cook for 15 minutes, or until rice is tender and all the water has been absorbed.

Let the rice stand for about 5 minutes before serving.

Sautéed Rice with Cashew Nuts

The cashew nut, which is now used in so many Indian dishes, is not native to Asia. Like so many interesting ingredients, it came to Europe from South America after the voyage of Columbus. The Portuguese probably introduced it to India, and it is a very important crop in the old Portuguese colony of Goa on the west coast. There, the trees grow wild as well as being cultivated, and the nut is even used to produce a very fiery, vodka-like alcoholic drink called "feni" – very much an acquired taste!

3 CUPS BASMATI RICE

2 TABLESPOONS CLARIFIED BUTTER

4 WHOLE CLOVES

4 WHOLE CARDAMOMS

2 WHOLE BAY LEAVES

1 TEASPOON SALT

1 GREEN CHILE, SLICED

2 RED CHILES, SLICED

⅓ CUP CASHEW NUTS

⅓ CUP GOLDEN RAISINS

4 CUPS WATER

Wash the rice and set it aside to drain.

Put the clarified butter in a heavy-bottom saucepan or deep skillet with a lid, add the whole cloves, cardamoms, bay leaves, salt, green and red chiles and sauté over a medium heat for about 2–3 minutes. Lower the heat and add the cashew nuts and golden raisins.

Using a slotted spoon, stir in the rice and stir-fry for about 2 minutes. Pour in the water and bring to a boil. Lower the heat, cover the pan and cook for 15–20 minutes, or until the rice is tender and water has been absorbed.

This rice dish is best served with a creamy curry.

PREVIOUS PAGES: *From left, Cabbage and Carrot Pulao (recipe page 98) and Sautéed Rice with Cashew Nuts (recipe above, right). Pulaos are one of the finest of all rice dishes and are typical of the Mogul influence on Indian cooking. Use Basmati rice wherever possible in the dishes in this chapter – its quality is, without doubt, the best available.*

Bay Rice
(Tez Pattay Kay Chawal)

A recipe using European bay leaves. They are a different species from the Indian variety, however. European bay leaves come from a tree which is a species of laurel, whereas the Indian variety comes from the cassia tree, and has a mysterious cinnamon-like scent. You can also try making this with Indian bay leaves.

2 CUPS BASMATI RICE

⅓ CUP (¾ STICK) BUTTER

1 TABLESPOON OIL

½ TEASPOON WHITE CUMIN SEEDS

3 CLOVES

6–8 BLACK PEPPERCORNS

4 GREEN CARDAMOMS

2 BAY LEAVES

1 TEASPOON SALT

3 CUPS WATER

Wash the rice, drain, and set aside. Melt the butter with the oil in a heavy-bottom saucepan, add the white cumin seeds, cloves, peppercorns, cardamoms and bay leaves and sauté over a medium heat for 1–2 minutes.

Add the salt and rice to the saucepan and stir-fry gently for about 1 minute, then pour in the water. Turn heat up to high and bring to a boil, reduce the heat to medium, cover the pan and cook for 15–20 minutes, or until the rice is tender and water has been absorbed.

Let the rice stand in the pan for 5 minutes before serving.

VARIATION
Bay Rice with Shredded Ginger
Ginger makes an interesting variation on this recipe.
Peel 1-inch of fresh ginger root and shred finely.
Add together with the other spices and proceed as in the main recipe.

Rice Cooked with Scallions

The proportion of rice to water is crucial in rice cooking so always use the same sized cup to measure rice and water.

2 CUPS BASMATI RICE

⅓ CUP (¾ STICK) BUTTER

1 TABLESPOON CORN OIL

½ TEASPOON FENNEL SEEDS

½ TEASPOON GINGER PULP

½ TEASPOON GARLIC PULP

1 TEASPOON SALT

1 LARGE SWEET RED PEPPER, DESEEDED AND DICED

2 SMALL BUNCHES SCALLIONS, CHOPPED

3 CUPS WATER

Wash the rice, drain into a strainer and set aside.

Heat the butter and oil in a heavy-bottom saucepan over medium heat, add the fennel seeds, ginger, garlic and salt and stir-fry for 1 minute.

Add half the sweet red pepper and all the scallions and stir-fry over medium heat for about 2 minutes.

Stir the rice in and stir-fry gently for about 1 minute.

Pour the water in and bring to a boil, lower heat to medium, cover the saucepan and cook for 15–20 minutes, or until the rice is tender and water has been absorbed.

Remove the lid to check if the rice is cooked and stir in the remaining diced sweet pepper before serving.

Idlis

Light, fluffy rice cakes, popular for breakfast with a pat of butter and honey or jam (not traditional, but wonderful!) – also delicious with curry sauces, dhaals, or spicy raitas. Steam them in patty pans, or dariole molds.

⅔ CUP URID DHAAL

1 TEASPOON SALT

1¾ CUPS PARBOILED RICE

CORN OIL FOR GREASING

Soak the urid dhaal for 1 hour, drain and place in a blender or food processor with salt. Blend to a paste.

Grind rice to a coarse powder, place in cheesecloth and rinse carefully. Set aside to soak for 10–15 minutes, then squeeze out excess moisture and mix with the lentil paste. Set aside in a warm place for 6 hours or overnight.

Grease the patty pans, spoon in the rice and lentil mixture, then steam over boiling water for about 10 minutes. Pierce with a skewer; the idlis are cooked when it comes out clean.

Vegetable Biryani

The "home" of the biryani is Hyderabad in south-central India, which was one of the great Mogul cities of India, and still has a very large Muslim population. This is one of the elegant dishes the Moguls brought with them – the product of the very sophisticated cooking of the courts of great emperors such as Akbar, Jehangir and Shah Jahan, who built the Taj Mahal as the tomb for his wife, Mumtaz. Though Mogul recipes like this were usually made with fish, chicken or lamb, the vegetarian version is equally splendid. Biryanis are cooked for special occasions, and the method is very interesting as the rice and vegetables are layered and saffron soaked in milk is poured over the top to make the rice partly colored. This recipe will serve six with side dishes.

2 ONIONS, SLICED

1 EGGPLANT, CUT INTO 6–8 PIECES

2 CARROTS, SLICED

½ CAULIFLOWER, CUT INTO SMALL FLOWERETS

½ CUP FRENCH BEANS, CUT INTO 1-INCH PIECES

½ CUP FROZEN PEAS

5 TABLESPOONS VEGETABLE GHEE OR CLARIFIED BUTTER

6 CARDAMOMS

4 WHOLE CLOVES

2 WHOLE CINNAMON STICKS

½ CUP GOLDEN RAISINS

½ CUP CASHEW NUTS

1 CUP PLAIN YOGURT

1½ TEASPOONS FRESH GINGER PULP

1½ TEASPOONS FRESH GARLIC PULP

1 TEASPOON BLACK CUMIN SEEDS

1 TEASPOON GARAM MASALA

2 TEASPOONS SALT

½ CUP GROUND ALMONDS

3½ CUPS BASMATI RICE

6¼ CUPS WATER

4 TABLESPOONS CHOPPED FRESH CILANTRO

⅓ CUP LEMON JUICE

3 GREEN CHILES, CHOPPED

1–2 TEASPOONS SAFFRON STRANDS,

CRUSHED AND SOAKED IN

⅔ CUP MILK

Wash and prepare all the vegetables.

In a large saucepan heat the ghee or clarified butter, add the onions and sauté until golden brown. Using a slotted spoon, remove half the onions and set aside in a bowl along with half the ghee.

Now add half of the whole spices – that is, the 3 cardamoms, 2 cloves and 1 cinnamon stick – and all the vegetables to the remaining onions and sauté them until soft. Add the golden raisins and cashew nuts.

Meanwhile, in a separate bowl mix the yogurt, ginger, garlic, cumin seeds, garam masala, half the salt and half the ground almonds. Pour this mixture over the vegetables and continue to stir-fry for a further 7–10 minutes. Remove the pan from the heat and set aside.

Wash the Basmati rice at least twice, handling it gently, then set aside to drain.

Into a large saucepan pour the measured water along with the remaining salt, half the fresh cilantro and the remaining black cumin seeds, cloves, cardamoms and cinnamon stick. Bring to a boil. Drain off any water from the rice in the bowl and transfer the rice to the boiling water in the saucepan. Bring to a boil and part-cook the rice. To check whether it is part-cooked, press a few grains between your thumb and forefinger. The rice should be soft on top and hard in the middle. Immediately the rice reaches this stage, drain it through a strainer. Divide the rice equally, leaving half in the strainer and spooning half into a saucepan.

Pour all the vegetable mixture over the top of the rice in the saucepan and garnish with half the cooked onions, ghee, fresh cilantro, lemon juice and half the green chiles.

Cover with the remaining rice, pour over the saffron in milk and garnish with the remaining ingredients.

Cover the saucepan first with tinfoil and then with a tight-fitting lid. Return the saucepan to the heat and cook over medium heat for 15–20 minutes, checking once to see that the rice is cooked right through. Let stand for 10–15 minutes. Mix gently with a slotted spoon before serving. A raita is usually served to complement the biryani, and at a dinner party, you could add a crunchy salad, such as Tomato and Onion Salad on page 111 or the Grated Mooli Salad on page 113. Serve also with crisp poppadums and a good, thick dhaal, such as Rasam or Toor Dhaal with Tomatoes, both on page 82.

VARIATION

A biryani can also be given the final cooking layered in a large bowl and cooked in a moderate oven. Once cooked, it can be turned out onto a dish as a mold.

RIGHT: *From top, the elegant, special occasion Vegetable Biryani (recipe above) together with the curry dish Vegetables in a Tangy Sauce (recipe page 38). Biryanis are yet another of the wonderful dishes introduced to India by the Moguls. This one, streaked with saffron is particularly elegant.*

Rice and Peas in Green Spices

(Haray Masalay Kay Chawal)

*"Chawal" means, simply "plain rice," and is complemented
here by peas and mint. It is astonishing how the same
"marriages" of ingredients occur in many different cuisines.
In Italian cooking, for instance, one of the great classics is
"risi e bisi" (rice and peas). Peas are often cooked with mint
in both French and English cooking.*

2 CUPS BASMATI RICE

¼ CUP PURE CLARIFIED BUTTER

1 LARGE BUNCH SCALLIONS, CHOPPED

1 TEASPOON GINGER PULP

1 TEASPOON GARLIC PULP

½ TEASPOON WHITE CUMIN SEEDS

3–4 GREEN CARDAMOMS, WHOLE

3 GREEN CHILES, CHOPPED

3 TABLESPOONS CHOPPED FRESH CILANTRO

1 TABLESPOON CHOPPED FRESH MINT LEAVES

¼ CUP FROZEN PEAS

¼ CUP PLAIN YOGURT

2 TEASPOONS SALT

3 CUPS WATER

Wash the rice at least twice, drain off the water and set the
aside in a bowl.

Heat the clarified butter in a medium-size saucepan, add the
scallions and sauté for about 2 minutes before adding the ginger, garlic, white cumin seeds, green cardamoms, green chiles,
fresh cilantro, mint and frozen peas. Lower the heat and stir-
fry for a further 2 minutes. Stir in the yogurt and continue to
stir-fry for another 2 minutes.

Add the rice and stir to mix together. Add the salt, pour in
the water, bring to a boil, lower the heat to medium, cover the
pan and cook for 15–20 minutes, or until the rice is tender and
water has been absorbed.

Let the rice stand for 5–7 minutes before serving with any of
the curries in this book.

Vegetable Rice

(Subzee Kay Chacoal)

*When serving this or other rice dishes with the curries in this
book, always allow the rice to stand for about
5 minutes before serving.*

5 TABLESPOONS OIL

8 CURRY LEAVES

6 GREEN CHILES, CHOPPED

1 ONION, SLICED

2 TOMATOES

½ TEASPOON GINGER PULP

½ TEASPOON GARLIC PULP

½ TEASPOON DRIED RED CHILES

½ TEASPOON TURMERIC

1 POTATO, DICED

1 CARROT, DICED

3 TABLESPOONS MOONG DHAAL

2 CUPS RICE

2 TEASPOONS SALT

3 CUPS WATER

⅓ TO ½ CUP LEMON JUICE

3 TABLESPOONS CHOPPED FRESH CILANTRO

Heat the oil in a heavy-bottom saucepan, add the curry leaves
and green chiles, and sauté for 2 minutes. Add the onion and
sauté for 2–3 minutes over medium heat. Gradually add the
tomatoes, ginger, garlic, dried red chiles, turmeric, diced
potato, carrots and moong dhaal.

Once all the ingredients are blended, continue stir-frying,
reducing the heat if necessary, for 2–3 minutes.

Now pour the rice in and continue to stir-fry the mixture in
semicircular movements.

Pour in the salt, water, lemon juice and fresh cilantro and stir
to mix together. Bring to a boil, lower the heat, cover the pan
and cook for 15–20 minutes, or until the rice is tender and
water has been absorbed,

Leave the rice to stand for 5–7 minutes before serving.

Saffron Rice with Peas
(Zafraan Aur Majar Pulao)

Saffron is one of the ingredients that indicates a Mogul origin in an Indian dish. It is made from the stigmas of the saffron crocus, which must be laboriously removed from the blossoms by hand – and this makes it a very expensive spice indeed. Some people substitute turmeric, but the only similarity will be the yellow color – the flavor is quite different, and the color is rather more "mustardy" than the clear golden orange of true saffron. In this dish, the saffron is poured in at the end, so the yellow appears as seams through the rice. This rice dish is garnished with delicious, crisp, golden-brown onions and fresh cilantro.

3 TABLESPOONS PURE CLARIFIED BUTTER

2 ONIONS, SLICED

1 TEASPOON WHITE CUMIN SEEDS

3 BLACK CARDAMOMS

1½-INCH PIECE OF CINNAMON STICK

2 CUPS RICE

¼ CUP PEAS

1½ TEASPOONS SALT

3 CUPS WATER

⅓ CUP MILK

½ TEASPOON SAFFRON STRANDS, CRUSHED

1 TABLESPOON CHOPPED FRESH CILANTRO

Melt the clarified butter in a heavy-bottom saucepan over a high heat, add onions, and sauté until crisp and golden brown.

Transfer half the onions into a bowl and reserve for garnish.

Lower the heat and add the whole spices to the saucepan, followed by the washed rice, peas and salt, stirring gently with a slotted spoon.

Pour in water and bring to a boil. Lower the heat, cover the pan and cook for 15–20 minutes, or until the rice is tender and water has been absorbed.

Meanwhile, heat the milk and add the saffron strands.

When the rice is cooked, pour the saffron milk over it and let the rice stand for a further 5 minutes before serving garnished with the crisp onions and fresh cilantro.

Pea Pulao
(Majar Pulao)

Pulaos, like biryanis, were introduced to India by the Moguls, and this method of cooking is one favored by them called "dum." Dum cooking is a little like French "daube," which can be cooked in the oven or on top of the stove – as long as the cooking vessel is tightly closed after the rice is brought to a boil. In this way, the ingredients are steamed to tenderness.

1 TABLESPOON CORN OIL

½ CUP (1 STICK) UNSALTED BUTTER

1 ONION, SLICED

3 WHOLE BLACK CARDAMOMS

6 WHOLE CLOVES

¼ TEASPOON BLACK CUMIN SEEDS

6–8 WHOLE BLACK PEPPERCORNS

1 TEASPOON GINGER PULP

1 TEASPOON GARLIC PULP

2 WHOLE BAY LEAVES

2 CINNAMON STICKS

½ CUP PLAIN YOGURT

½ CUP PEAS

3 POTATOES, CUT INTO WEDGES

1 TABLESPOON CHOPPED FRESH CILANTRO

2 GREEN CHILES, SLICED

2 CUPS BASMATI RICE

1 TEASPOON SALT

3 CUPS WATER

Heat the oil and butter in a medium-size saucepan. Add the onion, black cardamoms, whole cloves, black cumin seeds and black peppercorns and sauté until the onions are golden brown. Add the ginger, garlic, bay leaves and cinnamon sticks.

Meanwhile, whisk the plain yogurt lightly and pour onto the onions, followed by the peas and potatoes.

Stir-fry the mixture for a further 3 minutes, then pour in the remaining ingredients, except the water. Using a slotted spoon, mix the rice in gently, then stir-fry for about 2 minutes.

Pour in the water. Increase the heat to high and bring to a boil. Lower the heat to medium, cover the saucepan and cook for 15–20 minutes, or until the rice is tender and water has been absorbed.

Let the rice stand for 5–7 minutes before serving.

Pea and SweetcornPulao
(Matar Aur Bhutta Ka Pulao)

*Biryanis and pulaos always make wonderful party dishes,
as they can be prepared early in the day and covered with
tinfoil until needed. Place them in a preheated oven at
about 375°F for about 25–30 minutes before serving.*

2 CUPS BASMATI RICE

4 TABLESPOONS CLARIFIED BUTTER

½ TEASPOON BLACK CUMIN SEEDS

6–8 BLACK PEPPERCORNS

3 WHOLE CLOVES

3 GREEN CARDAMOMS

1-INCH PIECE OF CINNAMON STICK, CUT IN HALF

1 ONION, DICED

1½ TABLESPOONS SALT

1 TABLESPOON CHOPPED FRESH CILANTRO

2 GREEN CHILES, CHOPPED

2 BAY LEAVES

1 POTATO, DICED

¾ CUP PEAS

¼ CUP CORN

3 CUPS WATER

TOMATO SLICES, TO GARNISH (OPTIONAL)

Wash the rice, drain and set aside.

Heat the clarified butter in a heavy-bottom saucepan, add the
cumin seeds, black peppercorns, cloves, cardamoms and
cinnamon and sauté for about 30–40 seconds before adding
the onion. Continue cooking until the onion is golden brown.

Add the salt, cilantro, green chiles, bay leaves, potatoes, peas
and corn. Stir-fry for 3–5 minutes.

Mix in the rice, followed by the water. Bring to a boil, lower
the heat, cover the pan and cook for 15–20 minutes, or until
the rice is tender and the water has been absorbed.

Leave the rice to stand for a further 5 minutes before serving
garnished with sliced tomatoes, if you like.

VARIATION
Pea and Corn Pulao with Saffron
Soak a pinch of saffron strands in a little milk, then pour over
the pulao. Alternatively, mix the saffron with butter and dot
over the surface of the pulao.

Cabbage and Carrot Pulao
(Gobi Aur Gajar Ka Pulao)

*This is a very colorful dish with its orange flecks of carrot. In
India there is even a variety of carrot, available in winter,
which is such a deep, deep orange it is almost red.
They are particularly delicious when used to make halvas
(see recipes on page 120) – and very beautiful. I have
never seen these red carrots outside the subcontinent,
but you will find that this pulao is just as
colorful with ordinary carrots.*

2¼ CUPS BASMATI RICE

¼ CUP CLARIFIED BUTTER

2 ONIONS, SLICED

1 TEASPOON BLACK CUMIN SEEDS

4–6 GREEN CARDAMOMS

2-INCH PIECE OF CINNAMON STICK, HALVED

6 BLACK PEPPERCORNS

2-INCH PIECE FRESH GINGER, SHREDDED

1½ TEASPOONS SALT

½ SMALL WHITE CABBAGE, SHREDED

3 CARROTS, SHREDED

3¾ CUPS WATER

Wash the rice thoroughly and set aside in a strainer to drain.

Melt the clarified butter in a heavy-bottom saucepan, add the
onions, black cumin seeds, green cardamoms, cinnamon,
peppercorns, shredded ginger and salt and sauté until some
bits are darker than others.

Using a slotted spoon, stir the rice in, followed by the
cabbage and half the carrots.

Continue to stir-fry for about 3 minutes, then pour in the
water, bring to a boil, lower the heat to medium, cover the pan
and cook for 15–20 minutes, until the rice is tender and the
water has been absorbed.

Before serving the rice, stir in the remaining carrots.

Panir Pulao

Panir, also known as "paneer" is an important ingredient in vegetarian Indian cooking, and you may find it in an Asian specialty store. If you have difficulty in obtaining it, you will find a recipe for making your own in the chapter on curries, on page 74. It is a very versatile ingredient – you can dice it and sauté it until golden, as in this recipe, or crumble it so that it looks a little like ricotta or cottage cheese. I prefer it sautéd, as in this recipe, and it is easily adapted to other vegetable recipes if you would like to raise the protein content of a particular menu.

3 TABLESPOONS CLARIFIED BUTTER

¼ TEASPOON ONION SEEDS

¼ TEASPOON MUSTARD SEEDS

4 DRIED RED CHILES

¼ TEASPOON WHITE CUMIN SEEDS

4 CURRY LEAVES

1 ONION, SLICED

2 TOMATOES, SLICED

1 TABLESPOON FRESH CILANTRO

2 GREEN CHILES

1 TEASPOON SALT

2 CUPS RICE

3 CUPS WATER

½ CUP OIL

1½ CUPS PANIR, CUT INTO 1-INCH CUBES

Heat the clarified butter in a heavy-bottom saucepan over a medium heat, add the onion seeds, mustard seeds, dried red chiles, cumin seeds and curry leaves and sauté for about 1 minute. Add the onion and sauté until golden brown.

Stir in the tomatoes, fresh cilantro, green chiles, salt and rice and stir-fry for 1 minute using a slotted spoon. Pour in the water and bring to a boil, lower the heat, cover the pan and cook for 15–20 minutes, or until the rice is tender and the water has been absorbed.

Meanwhile, heat the oil in a skillet, add the panir cubes and sauté them until lightly browned. Remove the cubes from the pan with a slotted spoon and set aside on absorbent paper towels to drain.

When the rice is cooked, turn it out on to a serving dish and decorate with the panir cubes before serving.

Peas and Panir Pulao
(Matar Panir Pulao)

This pulao makes a delicious and impressive centrepiece for a special occasion meal. It is excellent served with Masala Corn Raita (see page 108).

1 CUP PLAIN YOGURT

½ CUP LIGHT CREAM

1½ TEASPOONS GARAM MASALA

1 TEASPOON GARLIC PULP

¼ TEASPOON TURMERIC

1 TEASPOON CHILE POWDER

½ TEASPOON BLACK CUMIN SEEDS

½ TEASPOON CARDAMOM SEEDS, CRUSHED

1 TEASPOON GINGER PULP

1½ TEASPOONS SALT

½ CUP PURE CLARIFIED BUTTER

3 CLOVES

2 BAY LEAVES

2 ONIONS, SLICED

3 TABLESPOONS TOMATO PASTE

¾ CUP PEAS

3 TABLESPOONS CHOPPED FRESH CILANTRO

¼ CUP LEMON JUICE

1½ CUPS PANIR, CUT INTO 1-INCH CUBES

2 CUPS RICE

3¾ CUPS WATER

1 TEASPOON SAFFRON STRANDS, CRUSHED

2 TOMATOES, SLICED

2 GREEN CHILES, CHOPPED

Whisk the yogurt and cream together and add the garam masala, garlic, turmeric, chile powder, black cumin seeds, crushed cardamom seeds, ginger and salt. Mix thoroughly and set aside.

Heat the clarified butter in a saucepan, add the cloves, bay leaves and onions. Sauté for 3 minutes, then lower the heat and add the tomato paste, peas, cilantro and lemon juice.

Next pour in the yogurt and spice mixture and cook, stirring occasionally, for 5–7 minutes. When the sauce has thickened, add the panir cubes, remove from the heat and set aside.

Wash the rice and tip it into a saucepan of lightly salted boiling water. Add the saffron strands. Partly cook the rice (so that it still has a "bone in the middle"). Drain the part-cooked rice into a strainer and set aside.

Line the bottom of a deep ovenproof dish with the sliced tomato and green chiles and pour the panir sauce in. Pour the rice on top of this and cover the dish with a tight-fitting lid or with tinfoil and cook in a preheated moderate oven, 350°F, for 15–20 minutes.

Remove from the oven and let stand for 5–7 minutes before removing the cover and turning out on a serving dish.

Breads

No Indian meal, especially in the north, is complete
without bread. There are many kinds in India, most
of them unleavened, that is, without yeast. The most
popular in the West is the leavened bread naan
(see page 34). This chapter includes a selection
of unleavened breads, including
chapatis and paratas.

Chapati

Chapatis are probably the best known of the Indian unleavened breads in the West. They are always circular, and measure about 6–7 inches in diameter. No fat is used in making the bread, which is cooked on a thawa, a cast-iron flat pan or griddle with a handle, available from Asian specialty stores. It is best to use a cloth, rolled up into a round shape, to move the chapati around on the thawa. In India chapatis are cooked on a naked flame so that they puff up. Allow about 2 per person.

3½ CUPS ATA (CHAPATI FLOUR)
1 TEASPOON SALT
1¼ CUPS WATER

Sift the flour into a deep bowl. Make a well in the center, add the salt and water, and mix together to form a soft dough.

Gather the dough from the sides of the bowl and knead with the back of your fist until the dough is pliable. Cover and let stand for about 10 minutes. Divide into 8 pieces and roll each one into a ball between the palms of your hands. Dust them with flour to prevent the dough sticking, and roll out to form a circle approximately 6 inches in diameter.

Heat the thawa to a very high temperature and add a chapati. After about 10–15 seconds, turn it over, pressing down with the cloth and moving the chapati around the thawa. Turn it over again and repeat, moving the chapati around. Make sure it is cooked, especially around the edges, then remove from the thawa. Repeat with the other chapatis.

Like all Indian breads, chapatis are best served as soon as possible after making. As they are cooked, keep them warm, covered in tinfoil, piled on top of each other. Brush each one with a little butter if you like, to help keep it moist.

Masala Puri

Puris are best cooked in a karahi and eaten straight away, usually with a curry. They may also be made with ordinary whole wheat flour instead of the traditional "ata," or chapati flour.

2 CUPS ATA (CHAPATI FLOUR)
1 TEASPOON SALT
½ TEASPOON ONION SEEDS
½ TEASPOON CRUSHED DRIED RED CHILES
1 GREEN CHILE, DICED
1 TABLESPOON CHOPPED FRESH CILANTRO
½ TEASPOON BAKING SODA
¾ CUP WATER
OIL FOR COOKING (SEE METHOD)

Sift the flour and salt into a deep bowl and make a well in the center. Mix in the onion seeds, the red and green chiles, cilantro and baking soda.

Gradually pour in sufficient water and, using your fingertips, mix to form a soft dough. Wipe the bowl clean with the ball of dough. Using the back of your hand, knead the dough for about 1 minute and let stand for 5–7 minutes.

Heat the oil, preferably in a karahi. Break small balls off the dough about the size of a golf ball and roll out on a lightly floured surface into 4–5 inch circular shapes.

Drop each puri into the hot oil, pressing down gently with a slotted spoon so that the puri is fully covered with oil. Gently turn it over, cook for a further 30 seconds, then remove. Drain off as much oil as possible back into the karahi and place the puri on a tray lined with paper towels to absorb any more oil.

Serve the puris immediately, allowing 2–3 per person.

Puri

2 CUPS ATA (CHAPATI FLOUR)
½ TEASPOON SALT
1 TABLESPOON OIL
½ TEASPOON BAKING SODA
⅓–½ CUP WATER
1¼ CUPS CORN OIL
½ CUP FLOUR, FOR DUSTING

Sift the flour into a deep bowl. Make a well in the center and add the salt, oil and baking soda. Stir in the measured water and, using your fingertips, gather in all the flour to form a soft pliable dough. Set aside.

Heat the oil in a karahi or deep skillet. Once the oil is hot, reduce the heat to medium. Break off small balls of dough, making about 12, and roll out on a lightly floured surface to 6-inch diameter rounds. Deep-fry the puris one by one, turning each at least once. Serve immediately.

PREVIOUS PAGES: *A selection of Indian breads, which are always best served hot, immediately after making. Clockwise from bottom left are Potato Roti – Aloo Ki Roti – (recipe page 103), Chapati (recipe above) and Stuffed Paratas (recipe page 103).*
ILLUSTRATED ON FRONTISPIECE: *Indian breads, including Besun Ki Roti (recipe page 103) and Chapatis.*

Stuffed Paratas

2 POTATOES, SLICED
1½ TEASPOONS SALT
2 GREEN CHILES, CHOPPED
½ TEASPOON CRUSHED RED CHILES
1 TEASPOON CHILE POWDER
2 TEASPOONS MANGO POWDER
1 TABLESPOON CHOPPED FRESH CILANTRO
3 TABLESPOONS FLOUR, FOR DUSTING
5–5 TABLESPOONS MELTED CLARIFIED BUTTER
PARATA DOUGH
3 CUPS CHAPATI FLOUR
1 TEASPOON SALT
WATER TO FORM A SOFT DOUGH (SEE METHOD)

Boil the potatoes until soft. Drain, then mash with the salt, chiles, chile powder, mango powder and cilantro. Set aside.

To make the dough, sift the flour and salt into a bowl, make a well in the center. Gradually add water, mixing it in with your fingers, to make a soft dough. Knead the dough on a flat surface, using your knuckles. Let stand for 10–15 minutes.

Break off balls slightly smaller than a tennis ball and make them into flat, round shapes, using the palm of your hand. On a lightly floured surface, roll the shapes out to about 6 inches. Put about a tablespoonful of the potato mixture into each parata and bring the edges together into the middle to make a round ball. Gently flatten it, then roll out to about a 10-inch round. Dust the parata with flour, if necessary.

Heat a thawa or flat griddle until it begins to steam. Gently lift a parata onto the thawa, pouring 1 teaspoon of clarified butter on top. With a flat spoon or spatula, turn the parata over and cook, slowly moving it about. Pour over another teaspoon of clarified butter and turn over again. Cook for 30 seconds, remove and serve with mango chutney, if you like.

Paratas

2½ CUPS ATA (CHAPATI FLOUR)
1 TEASPOON SALT
1¼ CUPS WATER
FLOUR FOR DUSTING
¼ CUP CLARIFIED BUTTER

Make the dough as above, divide into 6–8 portions and roll out on a floured surface. Brush the middle with ½ teaspoon clarified butter. Fold the dough in half and roll up into a tube. Flatten it with your palms, then coil round your fingers. Roll out to about 7 inch diameter, dusting with flour as necessary.

Heat a thawa or heavy-bottom skillet and slap a parata onto it (paratas should be cooked one at a time). Cook as in the previous recipe, moving, turning and brushing with clarified butter. Remove and keep warm until ready to serve.

Besun Ki Roti

Made with both ata (chapati flour) and gram flour (besun), then flavored with chile and cilantro, this roti is delicious with any of the curries in this book. Serve 2 per person.

1 CUP ATA (CHAPATI FLOUR)
¾ CUP GRAM FLOUR (BESUN)
½ TEASPOON SALT
1 TEASPOON CRUSHED DRIED RED CHILES
2 RED CHILES, FINELY CHOPPED
1 SMALL ONION, FINELY DICED
1 TABLESPOON CHOPPED FRESH CILANTRO
1 TEASPOON CHOPPED FRESH MINT
⅔ CUP WATER
3 TABLESPOONS CLARIFIED BUTTER

Sift the two flours and salt into a large bowl. With your fingers, mix in the dried and fresh chiles, onion, cilantro and mint.

Gradually stir in the water, form it into a soft dough and knead for about 5 minutes. Divide the dough into 8 portions. Roll out each portion of dough on a lightly floured surface to about 7 inches diameter.

Heat a thawa or heavy-bottom skillet. Pick each roti up gently and place it on to the thawa. Grease the top with about ½ teaspoon clarified butter and cook, turning it over 2–3 times or until you are sure the roti is cooked. Serve hot.

Potato Roti
(Aloo Ki Roti)

3 POTATOES
1 TEASPOON CRUSHED DRIED RED CHILES
2 GREEN CHILES, CHOPPED
1 TABLESPOON CHOPPED FRESH CILANTRO
1½ TEASPOONS MANGO POWDER
1 TEASPOON SALT
3 TABLESPOONS UNSALTED BUTTER, MELTED
1¼ CUPS ALL-PURPOSE FLOUR
CORN OIL FOR COOKING
FLOUR FOR DUSTING

Boil the potatoes, drain and mash. Mix in the dried and fresh chiles, cilantro, mango powder, salt and butter.

Gradually stir in the flour to form a soft dough. Divide into 6 pieces, then roll out to 5-inch rounds. Set aside.

Heat a thawa or a griddle, gently place a roti on to the thawa, drop about 1 teaspoon of oil around the edges and lift them gently so the oil slips under the roti. Pour another teaspoon of oil on top of the roti and gently turn it over.

When lightly browned, remove and set aside. Cook all the rotis in the same way and serve hot with curry or a dhaal.

Accompaniments

Mouth-watering side dishes are a traditional part of
almost every Indian meal, including breakfast.
Try raitas – cooling or spicy – chutneys, pickles, relishes
or kachumbers – as well as some unusual
salads and sauces.

Apple Chutney
(Seb Ki Chutney)

*No Indian meal is complete without a chutney or relish –
and they suit many western meals as well. They can be
sweet or sour, or both at the same time. They can also be
spicy or mild. They can be freshly made to eat immediately,
or bottled for future use, the way jelly and pickles are in
western cookery. There are many good ones available in
shops and supermarkets, but I think there's nothing to beat
the ones you make yourself.*

*Apples do not flourish in tropical climates, so the best apples
in India come from the state of Kashmir, which also
produces wonderful apple juice. Apple chutney is well-known
in Britain, where it was introduced by people who had come
to appreciate chutneys while working for the East India
Company or the military or Civil Service when India became
part of the British Empire. This one may be served as an
accompaniment to any of the curries in this book.*

2 LB GREEN APPLES

⅔ CUP WATER

¾ CUP BROWN SUGAR

½ TEASPOON GARAM MASALA

1 TEASPOON CHILE POWDER

1 TEASPOON GARLIC PULP

1¼ CUPS VINEGAR

1 TEASPOON SALT

1 TEASPOON CHOPPED FRESH MINT

Peel and dice the apples coarsely. Place them in a medium
saucepan and add the measured water.

In a small bowl, mix the brown sugar, garam masala, chile
powder, garlic, vinegar and salt together. Pour the mixture into
the saucepan and cook over a medium heat, mashing down the
apples occasionally, leaving some pieces whole so that the
apples are not completely mashed.

Once all the liquid is evaporated, add the chopped mint and
mix in well.

Transfer the chutney to a bowl to cool. Once it has cooled,
transfer it to a clean dry jar, cover and refrigerate. It will keep
for 2–3 days.

*PREVIOUS PAGES: From left, Plum Chutney (recipe page 107), Date
and Tamarind Chutney (recipe page 110) and Apple Chutney (recipe
above). Chutneys were enthusiastically adopted by the British under the
Raj, who took them back to England where they are now found in almost
every cupboard – the perfect way to enliven sandwiches and cold dishes.
They can be made more or less hot by varying the chile content.*

Hot Mint and Cilantro Chutney
(Mirch, Podinay Aur Haray Dhania Ki Chutney)

*This might be called a "fresh" chutney, since it is made just
before serving. It is very good with samosas and pakoras
and a dish of it on the table perks up the simplest meal. It is
best made in a food processor, as the ingredients need to be
blended well together. If you do not have one, then just chop
the fresh ingredients as finely as possible.*

4 TABLESPOONS CHOPPED FRESH MINT

4 TABLESPOONS CHOPPED FRESH CILANTRO

2 GREEN CHILES, FINELY CHOPPED

1 TEASPOON GARAM MASALA

½ TEASPOON CHILE POWDER

1 TEASPOON SUGAR

1 LEVEL TEASPOON SALT

3 TABLESPOONS LEMON JUICE

Mix all the ingredients, except the lemon juice, together with a
fork, or put them in a food processor and blend until smooth.

Tip the chutney into a bowl, stir in the lemon juice and serve.

Green Tomato Chutney

*If you grow your own tomatoes, this recipe is perfect for
using up end-of-season fruit which hasn't
ripened properly.*

2 LB GREEN TOMATOES, COARSELY CHOPPED

2 SMALL ONIONS, COARSELY CHOPPED

2 GREEN CHILES, FINELY CHOPPED

½ TEASPOON GINGER PULP

4 TABLESPOONS CHOPPED FRESH CILANTRO

1 LEVEL TEASPOON SALT

3 TABLESPOONS LEMON JUICE

Place the tomatoes and onions in a food processor. Add the
green chiles, ginger and cilantro and blend coarsely.

Spoon the chutney into a bowl and add lemon juice to taste.
Chill until ready to serve.

VARIATION
Green Mango Chutney
Substitute a similar quantity of green mango flesh – you will
need more than 2 lb because much of the weight of a mango is
in the seed.

Coconut Chutney

This is another "fresh" chutney, which should be served as soon as it is ready. It is quite popular in the south of India, where coconuts are widely grown, and is usually served with dosai (see recipe on page 22). Though it is nice to use freshly grated coconut for this chutney, ordinary shredded coconut is just as good.

3 TABLESPOONS CHANA DHAAL

2 CUPS SHREDDED COCONUT

½ TEASPOON GARLIC PULP

½ TEASPOON GINGER PULP

½ TEASPOON CRUSHED DRIED RED CHILES

1 TEASPOON SALT

2 GREEN CHILES, CHOPPED

1 TABLESPOON FRESH CILANTRO

4 TABLESPOONS LEMON JUICE

3 TABLESPOONS CORN OIL

4–6 CURRY LEAVES

½ TEASPOON MUSTARD SEEDS

½ CUP PLAIN YOGURT

Boil the chana dhaal in water to cover until soft enough to be mashed. Mash the dhaal with a wooden masher and set aside.

Put the coconut, garlic, ginger, crushed red chiles, salt, green chiles, fresh cilantro and lemon juice in a food processor or blender and grind for about 30 seconds. Add the mixture to the chana dhaal.

Heat the oil in a small skillet, add the curry leaves and mustard seeds and sauté for a minute or so, until they are a shade darker. Pour the hot oil with the seeds and leaves onto the coconut mixture. Stir in the yogurt and serve.

Plum Chutney

This is probably one of my favorite accompaniments. It is very versatile and, with its distinct sweet-and-sour flavor, goes well with almost any vegetarian Indian dish.

2 LB RED PLUMS

1 TEASPOON GINGER PULP

1 TEASPOON CHILE POWDER

2 TEASPOONS MANGO POWDER

1 TEASPOON GROUND CORIANDER

1 TEASPOON GROUND CUMIN

1 CUP BROWN SUGAR

1 TEASPOON SALT

1¼ CUPS VINEGAR

⅔ CUP WATER

½ CUP GOLDEN RAISINS

Cut the plums in half, remove and discard the pits. Chop the fruit coarsely and place them in a medium-size saucepan.

Blend together the ginger, chile powder, mango powder, ground coriander, cumin, brown sugar, salt, vinegar and water. Pour the mixture over the plums in the saucepan and bring to a boil.

Reduce the heat, add the golden raisins and cook, uncovered, until the plums are soft and all the liquid has been absorbed.

Transfer the chutney to a bowl and let cool. The plum chutney will keep for up to 4 weeks stored in covered jars in the refrigerator.

Mango Chutney

A wonderful way to serve India's favorite fruit. This version uses sweet, ripe mangoes. If you have green mangoes, follow the recipe for Green Tomato Chutney (page 106), rather than this one, substituting green mangoes for green tomatoes.

3 LARGE, RIPE MANGOES, SLICED

½ TEASPOON ASAFETIDA POWDER (OPTIONAL)

1-INCH PIECE OF FRESH GINGER, SHREDDED

1 TEASPOON CHILE POWDER

2 TEASPOONS MANGO POWDER

1 TABLESPOON CHOPPED FRESH MINT LEAVES

1 TEASPOON GROUND CUMIN

1 TABLESPOON BROWN SUGAR

1 TEASPOON SALT

LEMON JUICE (OPTIONAL)

Place all the ingredients in a food processor and blend briefly until mixed. Spoon into a serving dish, adding a little lemon juice if the mixture is too thick.

Eggplant Raita

Although raitas can be very cooling dishes to serve with spicy food, this one isn't, thanks to the fresh green chiles and dried red ones. To cool your palate, I include a recipe for cool Cucumber Raita below, right.

1 EGGPLANT, DICED

1 ONION, DICED

3 TABLESPOONS CORN OIL

½ TEASPOON ONION SEEDS

4 CURRY LEAVES

3 DRIED RED CHILES

2 GARLIC CLOVES

2 TOMATOES, DICED

2 GREEN CHILES, CHOPPED

1 TABLESPOON CHOPPED FRESH CILANTRO

1 TABLESPOON CHOPPED FRESH MINT LEAVES

¾ CUP PLAIN YOGURT

¾ CUP WATER

1 TEASPOON SALT

2 MINT SPRIGS, TO GARNISH

Set the prepared eggplant and onion dice to one side.

Heat the oil in a medium-size saucepan and sauté the onion seeds for about 30 seconds before adding the curry leaves, dried red chiles and garlic cloves. Sauté these for another minute, lowering the heat, if necessary.

Add the eggplant, onion and tomatoes to the saucepan and continue cooking for about 5 minutes, stirring occasionally.

Gradually add the green chiles, fresh cilantro and mint and stir to mix. Remove from the heat and set aside.

In a serving dish, beat the plain yogurt along with the water and salt.

Pour the eggplant mixture over the top of the yogurt and gently mix together.

Serve garnished with the mint sprigs.

Masala Corn Raita

Raitas are among the most versatile of all accompaniments. They can be served with almost any curry or meal. There are several ways raitas can be made, using ingredients such as cucumber, tomato, eggplant and onions.

2 TABLESPOONS CORN OIL

¼ TEASPOON ONION SEEDS

4 DRIED RED CHILES, WHOLE

1 SMALL ONION, CHOPPED

1½ CUPS CORN, CANNED OR FROZEN

1 TEASPOON CHILE POWDER

½ TEASPOON GROUND CORIANDER

1 TEASPOON SALT

3 TABLESPOONS CHOPPED FRESH CILANTRO

1¼ CUPS PLAIN YOGURT

6 CHERRY TOMATOES

SPRIG OF MINT

Heat the oil in a heavy-bottom saucepan over a medium heat and sauté the onion seeds, chiles and onion for about 1 minute. Add the corn, then the chile powder, ground coriander and salt. Sauté for about 2 minutes, stirring occasionally. Once all the liquid has been absorbed by the corn mixture, set the corn aside to cool for about 10 minutes.

Meanwhile, mix the fresh cilantro with the yogurt and set aside in a serving dish.

Pour the cooled corn into the yogurt and decorate with the cherry tomatoes and the mint sprig.

Cucumber Raita

This is the raita to cool the fires if you have been too enthusiastic with the chiles in other dishes. Try to find small cucumbers so that your raita will look more attractive. Yogurt is also very good for people with upset stomachs.

1¼ CUPS PLAIN YOGURT

1 CUCUMBER, SLICED, SALTED AND DRAINED

½ TEASPOON GROUND CUMIN

½ TEASPOON SALT

1 TEASPOON SUGAR

1 TEASPOON LEMON JUICE (OPTIONAL)

Beat the yogurt, stir in the cumin, salt and sugar, add the cucumber, taste and add lemon juice, if you like. Refrigerate the raita for at least 1 hour before serving.

RIGHT: *From top, Masala Corn Raita (recipe above, right) and Eggplant Raita (recipe above). Though raitas are often used as a cooling contrast to spicy curries, these two aren't – they are wonderfully spicy in their own right. If you would like a more cooling effect, try the Cucumber Raita (recipe right.)*

Tamarind and Sesame Seed Chutney
(Imli Aur Thill Ki Chutney)

Tamarind, or "imli," is a very popular flavoring in India – a little tart, like lime or lemon juice. This is a very typical Hyderabadi chutney. It makes a delicious accompaniment to a wide variety of dishes. It also makes a good base for salad sandwiches, and can be kept in the refrigerator for three or four days.

4 OUNCES RED TAMARIND BLOCK

¾ CUP HOT WATER

1 TEASPOON SUGAR

2½ CUPS SESAME SEEDS

2 GREEN CHILES, CHOPPED

3 TABLESPOONS CHOPPED FRESH CILANTRO

1 TEASPOON SALT

1 ONION, DICED

SPRIG OF FRESH CILANTRO

Place the tamarind block in the hot water and leave for about 15 minutes. Squeeze the pulp out and push through a strainer into a bowl to give a purée.

Add the sugar and set aside.

Dry-roast the sesame seeds in a small saucepan until they change color a little. Once they are cool, put them in a food processor and grind until powdery. Add the chiles, chopped cilantro, salt and half the onion and blend together.

Stir the blended spices into the tamarind pulp, adding a little water, if necessary, to loosen the mixture.

Pour the chutney into a serving dish and serve garnished with the remaining onions and the cilantro.

Date and Tamarind Chutney
(Imli Aur Khajoor Ki Chutney)

This chutney has a delicious and mouth-watering sweet-and-sour flavor, provided by the sweet dates and lemony tamarind. It is a very rich, dark brown, with a good, thick consistency. Serve it with any of the snacks or appetizers or as an accompaniment to any meal. Dates originated in the Persian Gulf, and probably came to India with the Moguls. They are very sweet, so there are a number of variations possible with this recipe, all involving very sweet, ripe fruits.

¼ CUP GOLDEN RAISINS

1¼ PITTED DATES

⅔ CUP HOT WATER

1 TABLESPOON RED TAMARIND PASTE

3 TABLESPOONS BROWN SUGAR

1 TEASPOON CHILE POWDER

2 TEASPOONS GROUND CORIANDER

1 TEASPOON GROUND CUMIN

1 TEASPOON SALT

1 TEASPOON GINGER POWDER

4 TABLESPOONS VINEGAR

Rinse the golden raisins and dates, drain and place in a saucepan with the hot water. Bring to a boil. Remove the pan from the heat and add the tamarind, brown sugar, chile powder, ground coriander, ground cumin, salt, ginger powder and vinegar.

Return to the heat and cook for about 1–2 minutes. Remove from the heat and let cool for about 10 minutes.

Place in a food processor and grind for about 30 seconds.

Transfer the chutney to a serving dish or jar. The chutney will keep in a jar for about a week.

VARIATIONS
Tamarind Chutney with Apricots, Apples or Peaches
This chutney may also be made substituting ½ lb of apricots or peaches, pitted, peeled and cut into chunks, or a similar quantity of apples, peeled, cored and quartered. Choose very ripe, fresh apricots, or the yellow variety of peaches, very ripe and soft. Apricots are native to China, but spread west to India. They were probably introduced into Europe after the conquests of Alexander the Great. They grow now in Kashmir, as do so many temperate zone fruits.

Illustrated on page 104.

Vadde

Vadde deep-fried dumplings are very popular in the northwestern state of Gujarat. They are wonderfully crunchy, spicy and very easy to make. Serve them either hot or cold. They are delicious as an appetizer, and equally good with other dishes. Always serve with a dipping sauce or chutney.

1 CUP URID DHAAL

½ BUNCH SCALLIONS, FINELY CHOPPED

1½ TEASPOONS CRUSHED CILANTRO

1 TEASPOON GINGER PULP

1 TEASPOON FENNEL SEEDS

½ TEASPOON BAKING SODA

1 TEASPOON SALT

4 GREEN CHILES, CHOPPED

3 TABLESPOONS FRESH CILANTRO

CORN OIL FOR DEEP-FRYING (SEE METHOD)

⅔ CUP COARSE SEMOLINA FLOUR

Soak the urid dhaal for several hours, preferably overnight. Drain thoroughly and blend to a purée in a food processor. Transfer the urid dhaal purée to a medium-size bowl.

Add the scallions, crushed cilantro, ginger pulp, fennel seeds, baking soda, salt, green chiles and fresh cilantro to the urid dhaal purée and mix together.

Press small balls of the mixture into rounds in the palms of your hands and make a hole in the middle of each one.

Heat the oil in a skillet, dip each vadde into the semolina flour, and sauté them in the hot oil, turning at least twice and gently pressing them down with the back of a spoon.

Once all the vadde are cooked, serve them hot with Spicy Tomato Ketchup (recipe page 117).

Tomato and Onion Salad

This combination is as popular in India as it is in the west – so common that you might overlook it as an accompaniment for a special occasion dinner party. Don't – it's very good!

4 RIPE TOMATOES

1 ONION, FINELY SLICED

1 TABLESPOON CHOPPED FRESH CILANTRO

1 LEMON, CUT INTO WEDGES, TO GARNISH (OPTIONAL)

Place the tomatoes on a serving dish and scatter over the onion and cilantro. Garnish with lemon wedges if you like.

VARIATION

Tomato and Onion Salad with Carrot and Lettuce

Add 2–3 lettuce leaves, finely shredded and 1 carrot, shredded or sliced, to the main recipe.

Banana and Coconut Salad

This salad couldn't be simpler – and is a very cooling accompaniment for a fiery curry. Never drink water if you find your curry was too spicy – it won't do any good at all. Instead, eat yogurt or a banana. Never keep bananas in the refrigerator – they don't like it. And don't keep them in the same fruit bowl as citrus fruit, because they will ripen and go soft much too quickly.

2 LARGE RIPE BANANAS

1 TABLESPOON LEMON JUICE

1 TABLESPOON SHREDDED COCONUT

Peel and slice the bananas into an attractive serving bowl. Brush with the lemon juice to prevent the bananas from browning, then sprinkle over the coconut.

Mooli and Carrot Salad
(Mooli Aurgajar Ki Salad)

Mooli, also known as Japanese radish, or "daikon," is from the same family as ordinary red garden radishes, and is now widely available. It is long, like a cucumber, white, and has a lovely crunchy flavor – milder than the red variety – and goes particularly well with carrots.

1 MOOLI, ABOUT 6–8 INCHES

2 CARROTS (ABOUT SAME WEIGHT AS MOOLI)

½ CUCUMBER

3 TABLESPOONS LIME JUICE

1 TABLESPOON HONEY

1 TEASPOON SALT

1 TEASPOON CHOPPED FRESH CILANTRO

1 TABLESPOON CHOPPED FRESH MINT

½ TEASPOON CRUSHED DRIED RED CHILES

2 RED CHILES, SLICED

Using the blade that shreds very finely in your food processor, shred the mooli and the carrots. Mix together and set aside. Wash and cut the cucumber into very thin 2-inch french fries.

Place the mooli, carrots and cucumber french fries on an attractive serving dish.

In a separate bowl, mix the lime juice, honey, salt, cilantro, mint and crushed red chiles together. Pour this mixture over the vegetables and serve garnished with sliced red chiles.

Fruit and Vegetable Salad

This is not exactly a typical Indian salad, but it may be a variation on coleslaw. Do try it any time of day, or as an appetizer.

8–10 BLACK SEEDLESS GRAPES, HALVED

8–10 WHITE SEEDLESS GRAPES, HALVED

2 BANANAS, SLICED

2 RED APPLES, DICED

½ CUCUMBER, SLICED

1 LARGE CARROT, SLICED

4 ICEBERG LETTUCE LEAVES, CHOPPED

1 CUP GREEK YOGURT

1 TEASPOON SUGAR

1 TEASPOON SALT

½ TEASPOON CHILE POWDER

½ TEASPOON GROUND CORIANDER

1 TABLESPOON CHOPPED FRESH MINT

¼ CUP WALNUTS, HALVED

SPRIG OF MINT

Place the prepared fruit and vegetables in a glass bowl.

Mix together the yogurt, sugar, salt, chile powder, ground coriander and chopped mint. Pour the yogurt mixture over the salad and mix in gently.

Garnish the salad with the walnuts and the sprig of mint and serve chilled.

VARIATION

Banana, Coconut and Lemon Salad

Instead of the grapes and apples in the main recipe, substitute 2 ripe bananas, 1 tablespoon sweet shredded coconut and 1 tablespoon lemon juice. Proceed as in the main recipe.

Grated Mooli Salad

Mooli – also known as "daikon" or Japanese radish – is widely available in Asian specialty stores, and bigger supermarkets. It is often eaten sliced on its own as a salad accompaniment. In this recipe the mooli is shredded and served in a yogurt sauce garnished with seasoned oil.

1½ LB MOOLI, SHREDDED

1¼ CUPS PLAIN YOGURT

1 TEASPOON SUGAR

1 TEASPOON SALT

1 TABLESPOON FRESH CILANTRO

1 TABLESPOON FRESH MINT

2 FRESH RED CHILES, CHOPPED

⅔ CUP WATER

1 TABLESPOON OIL

¼ TEASPOON MUSTARD SEEDS

4 CURRY LEAVES

TO GARNISH

PINCH OF GROUND CUMIN

PINCH OF GROUND CORIANDER

PINCH OF CHILE POWDER

Put the shredded mooli aside in a serving dish.

Beat together the yogurt, sugar, salt, cilantro, mint, chopped chiles and water and pour over the mooli.

Heat the oil in a small pan and sauté the mustard seeds and curry leaves in the hot oil until they turn a shade darker. Pour the oil (and the seeds and curry leaves) on the yogurt while still hot. Sprinkle over the cumin powder, coriander powder and chile powder.

VARIATION

Mooli Salad with Coconut and a Spicy Dressing

Add 1 tablespoon shredded coconut to the above recipe. Mix ⅔ cup corn oil with 1 tablespoon onion seeds and ¼ teaspoon crushed dried red chiles, then spoon over the salad. Keep any surplus oil dressing in a screwtop jar in the refrigerator.

LEFT: *From top, Fruit and Vegetable Salad (recipe above) and Grated Mooli Salad (recipe above, right). Salads are as important in Indian cooking as in western cuisine, providing a delicious contrast in flavor and texture. Both these recipes can be varied according to which fruits and vegetables are in season.*

Sweet and Sour Tomato and Onion Relish

This is a very versatile and delicious accompaniment.

3 TABLESPOONS CORN OIL

2 TEASPOONS BROWN SUGAR

2 GARLIC CLOVES, HALVED

1 ONION, CHOPPED

SALT TO TASTE

¼ TEASPOON CRUSHED DRIED RED CHILES

1 FRESH GREEN CHILE, CHOPPED

4 TABLESPOONS VINEGAR

2 TOMATOES, DESEEDED AND SLICED

1 SWEET GREEN PEPPER, DESEEDED AND SLICED

1 TABLESPOON CHOPPED FRESH CILANTRO

Heat the oil in a deep skillet over a medium heat, lower the heat and sprinkle in the brown sugar. Sauté it lightly.

Add the garlic cloves, followed by the onion. Continue cooking for about 2 minutes. Add the salt, crushed red chiles and green chile and stir-fry.

Reduce the heat and pour the vinegar into the pan, then add the tomatoes, sweet green pepper and fresh cilantro and continue to stir-fry for a further 3–5 minutes.

Transfer the relish to an attractive serving dish. It may be served hot or cold.

RIGHT: *From top, Onion and Cucumber Relish (recipe right) and Sweet and Sour Tomato and Onion Relish (recipe above). Relishes, like chutneys, were "borrowed" from India and adapted to British cooking by people who had worked for the British East India Company, or later for the military or civil service when India became part of the British Empire. Englishmen developed a taste for spice and curry, and these delicious concoctions seemed to add flavor and interest to the bland foods of their native England. In India, relishes are used as a contrast to more substantial dishes, such as curries.*

Onion Relish

Use small onions for this relish as they make a better-looking salad when the onions are cut into rings. There are many varieties in India, ranging from the shallot types in the south, to the small, round, red ones in the north. Onions are served with most meals in Indian households except in the prosperous and vegetarian Jains community, who eat no root vegetables of any kind.

3 TABLESPOONS CHOPPED FRESH MINT

3 TABLESPOONS CHOPPED FRESH CILANTRO

1 GREEN CHILE, CHOPPED

1 RED CHILE, CHOPPED

½ TEASPOON SALT

4 SMALL ONIONS

1 LIME

½ TEASPOON BLACK PEPPERCORNS, CRUSHED

Mix the chopped mint, cilantro, green and red chiles and salt together in a bowl.

Peel the onions, cut in rings and place on a serving dish.

Cut the lime in four quarters and squeeze the juice from two of them onto the onions. Stir the mint mixture into the onions and sprinkle the crushed black peppercorns over the top.

Garnish with the remaining lime quarters.

Onion and Cucumber Relish

Relishes are an important part of any meal as they not only help to perk it up but also help turn an ordinary meal into an interesting one.

1 LARGE BUNCH SCALLIONS, FINELY CHOPPED

1 ONION, FINELY DICED

1 CUCUMBER, FINELY DICED

1 TABLESPOON CHOPPED FRESH MINT

1 TABLESPOON CHOPPED FRESH CILANTRO

3 TABLESPOONS LEMON JUICE

½ TEASPOON SALT

2 RED CHILES

CRUSHED BLACK PEPPERCORNS

TO GARNISH

SPRIG OF CILANTRO

SPRIG OF MINT

Mix the scallions, onion, cucumber, mint and cilantro together. Add the lemon juice and salt and mix thoroughly.

Mix in the red chiles and sprinkle on the black pepper. Serve the dish garnished with the cilantro and mint.

114

Onion and Red Pepper Kachumber

Kachumbers are the quickest and easiest of salads. This one is crunchy and fresh.

1 ONION, FINELY CHOPPED
½ SWEET RED PEPPER
½ SWEET YELLOW PEPPER
1 TABLESPOON CHOPPED FRESH CILANTRO
1 TEASPOON SESAME SEEDS
½ TABLESPOON LEMON JUICE

Deseed the peppers and chop them finely. Place in a serving bowl and mix in the onion and cilantro. Sprinkle with sesame seeds and lemon juice. Serve immediately.

VARIATION
Kachumber with Chick peas, Tomato, Onion and Peppers
Add 1 large, sliced tomato and a few tablespoons of canned chick peas, if you like, to the recipe above. Serve immediately.

Guava Kachumber

Guavas are becoming more widely available in larger supermarkets, and you will certainly find them in Asian and Oriental specialty stores. Their scent, when ripe, is utterly wonderful – it's worth buying them and just keeping them in a fruit bowl to enjoy their fragrance. Better than roses! They are usually eaten fresh, but they make a delicious kachumber. This one can be eaten by itself, like a chaat.

6 GUAVAS
1 TEASPOON RED CHILE POWDER
3 TABLESPOONS LEMON JUICE
½ TEASPOON SALT
2 TEASPOONS SUGAR
FRESHLY GROUND BLACK PEPPER
1 TABLESPOON CHOPPED FRESH MINT, TO GARNISH

Do not peel the guavas, or you will lose their lovely scent. Chop into large dice, or slice like tomatoes. Sprinkle over the chile powder, lemon juice, salt and sugar, and mix gently. Sprinkle with freshly ground black pepper and the chopped fresh mint, to garnish.

VARIATION
Banana Kachumber
Substitute 2–3 ripe bananas, sliced, for the guavas, and then proceed as in the main recipe.

Bundi in Masala Yogurt

Bundi, which is made from lentil flour, is widely available from Indian and Pakistani specialty stores. It is used to make this yogurt-based accompaniment, which is delicious and versatile.

1 CUP PLAIN YOGURT
1 TEASPOON SALT
1 TABLESPOON SUGAR
¼ CUP WATER
½ TEASPOON GROUND CORIANDER
½ TEASPOON CHILE POWER
1 TABLESPOON CHOPPED FRESH CILANTRO
1 TABLESPOON OIL
¼ TEASPOON ONION SEEDS
¼ TEASPOON WHITE CUMIN SEEDS
3 DRIED RED CHILES
½ CUP BUNDI

Beat the yogurt and add the salt, sugar, water, ground coriander, chile powder and chopped cilantro and set aside.

Heat the oil in a small skillet and sauté the onion seeds, white cumin seeds and dried red chiles. Remove from the heat and set aside for a few seconds while you pour the bundi into the yogurt and mix it in well.

Pour the oil dressing over the yogurt mixture and serve. NOTE: You may immerse the bundi in hot water for a few seconds to soften it before adding it to the yogurt.

Spicy Dip

Another dip to use with appetizers, or with poppadums or nibbles at a drinks party.

1 CUP GREEK YOGURT
1 GREEN CHILE, CHOPPED
1 TEASPOON SALT
1 TABLESPOON FRESH CILANTRO
½ CUCUMBER, COARSELY CHOPPED
½ CUP LIGHT CREAM
1 TEASPOON FRESH MINT LEAVES
TO GARNISH
SPRIG OF MINT
SPRIG OF CILANTRO

Place the Greek yogurt, chile, salt, fresh cilantro, cucumber, light cream and fresh mint in a food processor and whisk for about 40 seconds.

Transfer to a serving bowl and serve garnished with the mint and cilantro.

Hot Mango Pickle

Unripe or green mangoes should be used for pickles. They usually arrive in the shops in this state, so choose the greenest you can find. Pickles are usually quite hot, and so should be eaten in very small quantities.

5 LARGE UNRIPE MANGOES, UNPEELED

3 TABLESPOONS SALT

4–5 TABLESPOONS CORN OIL

½ TEASPOON ONION SEEDS

½ TEASPOON MUSTARD SEEDS

¼ TEASPOON FENUGREEK SEEDS

¼ TEASPOON CRUSHED CORIANDER SEEDS

¼ TEASPOON WHITE CUMIN SEEDS

¼ TEASPOON FENNEL SEEDS

¼ TEASPOON CRUSHED DRIED RED CHILES

1-INCH PIECE FRESH GINGER, SHREDDED

2 CURRY LEAVES

1 TEASPOON CHILE POWDER

¼ TEASPOON TURMERIC

1½ TEASPOONS GROUND CORIANDER

1 TEASPOON SALT

Wash the mangoes and cut into 1-inch pieces, discarding the seeds. Rub the salt on the pieces and leave overnight. Squeeze out all the liquid from the pieces, then leave to dry for a minimum of 6 hours.

Heat the corn oil and sauté all the whole spices for about 1 minute.

Remove from the heat and add the chile powder, turmeric, ground coriander and salt. Blend everything together, then add the mango pieces. Return to the heat and stir-fry for about 2 minutes.

Set aside to cool, then store in airtight containers.

Spicy Tomato Ketchup

This dip can be served as an appetizer with vegetable crudités, or as an accompaniment to other dishes.

½ CUP KETCHUP

1 TEASPOON LEMON JUICE

½ TEASPOON CHILE POWDER

SALT

1 TEASPOON FINELY CHOPPED FRESH CILANTRO

Mix all the ingredients together and serve.

Eggplant Bhurta

Beautiful, glossy purple eggplants are native to India, and were taken to Europe as early as the 14th century. There is also a white form, which gave rise to their name. They range in size from the heavy, large ones used in this recipe, to long thin curved ones – which look pretty when used in vegetable dishes – to little round white ones, just like large hens' eggs. Bhurta is eaten as an accompaniment all over India, but perhaps more in the north. Though it can be made with other vegetables, eggplants are probably the most popular.

1 LARGE EGGPLANT

SALT

1 TEASPOON SALT

3 GREEN CHILES, FINELY CHOPPED

1 ONION, FINELY CHOPPED

2 TOMATOES, FINELY CHOPPED

3 TABLESPOONS OIL

½ TEASPOON ONION SEEDS

4 CURRY LEAVES

¾ CUP PLAIN YOGURT

3 TABLESPOONS CHOPPED FRESH CILANTRO

3 TABLESPOONS CHOPPED FRESH MINT

Peel the eggplant, chop coarsely and cook in lightly salted boiling water until soft and mushy. Drain the eggplant well and place on a serving dish.

Mix the chiles, onion and tomatoes into the eggplant.

Heat the oil in a small pan, add the onion seeds and curry leaves and sauté for 2–3 minutes, or until they turn a shade darker. Pour the hot, spiced oil over the eggplant.

Beat the yogurt and add the cilantro and mint. Pour the mixture over the bhurta.

VARIATION

Cucumber Bhurta, Doodhi or Marrow Bhurta

Other vegetables may be used instead of the eggplant. Replace the eggplant with a doodhi or marrow, or 2 large cucumbers, and proceed as in the main recipe.

Desserts

Desserts and sweetmeats are most often served as special dishes for festive occasions like weddings and other family celebrations. While this chapter includes two recipes for halva, the sweetmeat for religious festivals, there are also more everyday sweet rice dishes, and a recipe for lassi, the cooling yogurt-based drink.

Chana Dhaal Halva

This is a traditional recipe, made quite regularly in some Muslim households. It is also stuffed in puris and the puris are then sautéd and served with kheer (rice pudding). However, served on its own as a dessert it is delicious.

2 CUPS CHANA DHAAL
3¾ CUPS WATER
6 TABLESPOONS PURE CLARIFIED BUTTER
3 GREEN CARDAMOMS, CRUSHED
4 WHOLE CLOVES
1½ CUPS GROUND ALMONDS
1¼–1½ CUPS SUGAR
1 TEASPOON SAFFRON STRANDS
½ CUP GOLDEN RAISINS
SLIVERED ALMONDS, TO GARNISH

Wash the dhaal and pick over for any stones, etc. Place in a medium heavy-bottom saucepan with the water. Bring to a boil, lower the heat and cook until the dhaal is soft enough to be mashed.

Drain well and discard the water, then transfer the dhaal to a blender or food processor and blend to form a paste-like consistency. If necessary, add up to ⅔ cup water to form the required consistency.

Heat the clarified butter in a large saucepan, then add the crushed cardamom seeds and cloves. Lower the heat and add the chana dhaal paste and start stirring and mixing together gently, using the bhoono-ing method (see page 9).

Continue to stir-fry, scraping the bottom of the pan, for about 5–7 minutes. Gradually fold the ground almonds into the mixture and continue to stir-fry for a further 5–7 minutes.

Next fold in the sugar, saffron and golden raisins. Mix well.

The halva should now have become darker. Continue to stir-fry for another 2 minutes. Remove the pan from the heat and transfer to a serving dish.

Decorate the halva with slivered almonds. It may be served hot or cold, with cream if you like.

Almond and Semolina Halva
(Badam Aur Sooji Ka Halva)

1¼–1½ CUPS SUGAR
4½ CUPS WATER
¼ CUP PURE CLARIFIED BUTTER
3 GREEN CARDAMOMS
2 CLOVES
1¼ CUPS COARSE SEMOLINA
1½ CUPS GROUND ALMONDS
½ TEASPOON SAFFRON STRANDS
⅓ CUP GOLDEN RAISINS
TO GARNISH
1 TABLESPOON SLIVERED ALMONDS
1 TABLESPOON PISTACHIO NUTS
2 SHEETS VARQ

Place the sugar and 2 cups of the water in a large saucepan and bring to a boil. Continue to boil until forms a thick syrup.

Meanwhile, melt the clarified butter in a heavy-bottom saucepan. Add the cardamoms and cloves and stir-fry for about 10 seconds.

Mix the semolina and almonds together and add them to the hot clarified butter. Lower the heat to medium. Stir-fry for about 5 minutes. Add the saffron strands and golden raisins and stir-fry for a further 2 minutes.

Pour in the remaining water and cook over a low heat, stirring occasionally.

Once the syrup is ready, pour it into the halva and cook until the syrup is fully absorbed and the halva is a golden color.

Transfer the halva to a serving dish and serve garnished with the almonds, pistachio nuts and varq. Serve the halva with cream, too, if you like.

Lassi

This delightfully cool drink makes a refreshing accompaniment to hot and spicy curries. The saffron flavoring is unusual but delicious.

1¼ CUPS PLAIN YOGURT
2½ CUPS WATER
⅓–½ CUP SUGAR
LARGE PINCH OF POWDERED SAFFRON,
PLUS EXTRA TO DECORATE

PREVIOUS PAGES: *From left, Saffron Kheer (Zafrani Kheer), (recipe page 121), and Almond and Semolina Halva (Bedam aur Sooji Ka Halva), decorated with almonds and pistachios (recipe above, right). Indians have an incorrigibly sweet tooth, especially for sweetmeats. These desserts are just a selection of the many marvellous puddings to be found in the various regional Indian cuisines.*

Put the yogurt in a jug and whisk with a wire whisk for about 2 minutes. Pour in the water, sugar and saffron and continue to whisk for a further 3–5 minutes.

Serve the lassi chilled with an extra pinch of saffron sprinkled over the top.

Ground Rice Pudding
(Firni)

⅓ CUP GROUND RICE
½ CUP GROUND ALMONDS
3¾ CUPS MILK
2 CARDAMOM SEEDS, CRUSHED
½–¾ CUP SUGAR
1 TEASPOON KEWRA WATER (OPTIONAL)
TO GARNISH
4–6 PISTACHIO NUTS, SLICED
4–6 ALMONDS, SLIVERED
2 VARQ LEAVES (OPTIONAL)

Mix the ground rice and ground almonds together. Pour into a saucepan and gradually add 2½ cups of the milk, beating continually to prevent any balls forming.

Add the cardamom seeds and cook over a low heat for at least 15 minutes, stirring occasionally.

Add the sugar and the remaining milk. Continue to cook, stirring occasionally to prevent the mixture from catching on the bottom of the pan, until it has thickened.

Once the pudding has thickened to about the consistency of a thick vegetable soup, stir in the kewra water, if using, and transfer the pudding to a serving dish. Garnish with the pistachio nuts, almonds and varq, if using.

The pudding may be served hot or cold.

Gujarati-style Rice Pudding

¼ CUP BASMATI RICE
5 CUPS MILK
½ CUP GROUND ALMONDS
4 GREEN CARDAMOMS
5 TABLESPOONS SUGAR
¼ CUP SLIVERED ALMONDS, TO DECORATE

Wash the rice thoroughly. Drain and set aside. Pour the milk into a large saucepan and bring to a boil. Add the rice and cook over a medium heat for about 10 minutes. Add the ground almonds and cardamoms and cook until the milk is reduced to half its quantity.

Add the sugar and continue cooking, stirring, for a further 5 minutes.

Transfer the pudding to a serving dish, decorate with slivered almonds and serve. The cardamoms may be removed before serving, but this is not necessary.

Saffron Kheer
(Zafrani Kheer)

½ CUP BASMATI RICE
2 TABLESPOONS PURE CLARIFIED BUTTER
3 GREEN CARDAMOMS
1 TABLESPOON GROUND ALMONDS
1 TEASPOON SAFFRON STRANDS
6¼ CUPS WHOLE MILK
⅔–¾ CUP SUGAR
TO GARNISH
¼ CUP FLAKED ALMONDS
1 OR 2 VARQ LEAVES (OPTIONAL)

Coarsely grind the rice in a food processor and set aside.

Heat the clarified butter in a large saucepan and sauté the cardamoms for a few seconds. Lower the heat, add the ground almonds, rice and the saffron strands and stir-fry for about 1 minute.

Remove the pan from the heat and pour in the milk, stirring continuously to prevent any balls forming. Return to the heat and bring to a boil. Lower the heat and cook until reduced by half. Add the sugar and cook for 5–7 minutes more, stirring occasionally to prevent it from sticking to the pan.

Remove from the heat, transfer a serving dish and garnish with the almonds and varq leaves, if using.

Coconut and Rice Payasham

½ CUP BASMATI RICE
6¼ CUPS MILK
½ TEASPOON CRUSHED CARDAMOM SEEDS
1⅓ CUPS SHREDDED COCONUT
1–1¼ CUPS SUGAR
4 TABLESPOONS ROSEWATER
8–10 PISTACHIO NUTS, CHOPPED
10–12 FLAKED ALMOND PIECES

Wash the rice, drain well and place in a medium saucepan with 3¾ cups of the milk, the cardamoms and coconut.

Place the pan, partly covered, over medium heat and cook for 35–40 minutes, or until the rice is soft enough to be mashed and most of the milk has been absorbed. Remove from the heat, mash the rice, add the sugar and the remaining milk.

Return to the heat and bring to a boil, stirring occasionally. Continue cooking for 5–7 minutes then pour in the rosewater.

Transfer to a heatproof dish. Decorate with the pistachio nuts and flaked almonds. Serve chilled.

Equipment

You probably already have in your kitchen almost all the equipment you will need for cooking Indian food. Good-quality, heavy-bottom saucepans and a skillet, some wooden spatulas and a slotted spoon for stirring rice, are the first essentials. If you have a Chinese wok, that can also be a good substitute for the karahi or balti pan.

You should also have good, sharp knives, kitchen scales, measuring spoons and a measuring jug.

In an Indian kitchen you would probably also find a rice cooker and perhaps a garlic press, as well as more traditional equipment. Suggestions are:

Thawa

A slightly concave griddle or skillet, usually made of cast-iron, is used for cooking chapatis and paratas and for roasting spices. An ordinary skillet makes the perfect substitute – use a small one, about 5 inches, for dry-roasting spices (see page 8).

Karahi

Sometimes spelled *karihai* or *kadhai*. This is a deep skillet which resembles a straight-sided wok, with handles on both sides. It is made from various metals and alloys, the most common of which are iron, aluminum and stainless steel. You can substitute a Chinese wok or a good-quality, large skillet.

Balti pans

Balti cooking is becoming increasingly popular, and balti pans are now widely available. They are almost identical to the karahi, though their name means "bucket." If you don't have an authentic balti pan, a wok, karahi or deep skillet makes a perfectly acceptable substitute.

Girda

A small pastry board, 10 inches in diameter, with short legs, used for rolling out dough. You can substitute an ordinary wooden cutting board, or your normal surface for working dough.

Food Processor or Blender

Traditionally, Indian households would use a grinding stone for preparing spices and grinding flours. In modern kitchens, these tasks have been taken over by the food processor and blender.

Spice Grinder

A traditional Indian cook would grind her spices on the grinding stone. You could substitute a mortar and pestle or a rolling pin, but the best modern substitute in both Asian and western kitchens is a coffee grinder, kept just for grinding spices (otherwise coffee ground in it would acquire a rather peppery, spicy taste). A food processor is just too large to cope with the small quantities of spices needed for home-cooked curries.

Spice box

An Indian cook keeps spices in a Spice Box beside the stove. She uses spices every day and so uses them quickly, before they have time to go stale. You should buy small quantities and keep them in airtight bottles in a cool, dark place. You could also keep them, tightly sealed, in the refrigerator if you have space.

Rolling pin

For rolling out chapati and other doughs. In many Indian households, the flat, heavy grindstone and a *mussal*, which is rather like a rolling pin, are used.

Garlic press

Use a garlic press if you have one. Alternatively, crush the cloves with the flat of a large knife and remove the papery covering. Drop a few grains of salt over the smashed clove and mash carefully with the flat, pointed end of a knife. The clove will be puréed in a matter of seconds, with no waste. For puréeing larger amounts of garlic see page 9.

Rice cookers

Electric rice cookers have become popular throughout the East, wherever rice is cooked regularly and in large quantities, because they ensure that the rice is always perfectly cooked and will stay warm until required, without burning. They aren't absolutely essential, but if you cook rice often I think it's worth buying one.

RIGHT: *From the top, Panir and Vegetable Roghan Josh (recipe page 70), and Stir-fry Cabbage with Green Mango (recipe page 71). Unusual vegetable combinations give extra interest to these curries.*

Index

Page numbers in *italic* refer to the illustrations

124